Endorsements for

Daniel: Esteemed by God

"Although raised in a very austere Mennonite home, I have always been fascinated by wonder, awe, and mystery—the parts of my faith I could not fully understand. And my namesake book of Daniel shares wonderful stories of God speaking through dreams and visions. I love knowing we are seeing only the tip of the iceberg in understanding God—and even the world in which we live. *Daniel: Esteemed by God* is a welcome and refreshing guide to understanding more of the tiny divine insights we are privileged to experience, if we have our spiritual eyes, ears, and minds attuned for the reception."

—**Dan Miller**, author and coach at 48Days.com

"The book of Daniel can feel overwhelming. Honestly, it hasn't been one of my 'favorites' to read; however, after reading this book, I found the book of Daniel to be really interesting from many perspectives. I especially appreciate how the author discusses the book of Daniel and makes it relevant to 'everyday people.'"

—**Jen McDonough** (aka The Iron Jen), speaker, trainer, and author at theironjen.com

"Marilynn leads readers on a fascinating, easy-to-read journey through time. As she lays out the historical background for Daniel, she presents this biblical hero's difficulties in a way that feels as fresh and modern as any problem you or I might face today. For me, it read like a suspense novel I could not put down!"

—**Cara Polk**, wellness strategist at livingwelldesigns.com

"While we all seek to know, cherish, and glorify God more, with limited understanding of biblical facts and truth, it's easy to come up short. Thankfully, through the power of His Word, we have both the opportunity and the responsibility to grow and mature in our walk. Marilynn Hood does a brilliant job of sharing her perspective on Daniel and the events surrounding his life. Her understanding and writing comes from a pure and undiluted place of wanting to know and grow more. The layout and short chapters of this book make it an excellent choice for individual, group, and congregation-wide study."

—**Joel Boggess**, speaker, author, podcaster at relaunchshow.com

"*Daniel: Esteemed by God* is anything but a dry, historical accounting of an Old Testament book. It's a walk with the people through the events they faced, and it takes you right into the story as if you are experiencing it yourself. Is it historically and biblically accurate? Yes, but it reads more like an engaging novel than a crusty textbook. A great addition for your library!"

—**Kent Julian**, professional speaker and consultant at LiveItForward.com

"Daniel is one of my favorite biblical heroes. This young man, who lost so much, sparkles against the dark and challenging circumstances of his life. Marilynn Hood sets the stage for understanding Daniel by providing the background and prophesies leading up to this somber period of Israel's exile. She masterfully shows the hand of God at work in Daniel and how that same hand is at work for us. The short chapters and personal applications make this book appropriate for individual and group study. *Daniel: Esteemed by God* is a book for our times."

—**Debbie W. Wilson**, speaker, author of *Little Women, Big God* and blogger at debbiewwilson.com

Daniel: Esteemed by God

Finding Peace in a Changing World

by Marilynn E. Hood

Daniel: Esteemed by God
© 2017 by Marilynn E. Hood

All rights are reserved. No part of this publication may be reproduced in any form or by any electronic or mechanical means, including information storage and retrieval systems, without permission in writing by the publisher, except by a reviewer who may quote brief passages in a review. For information regarding permission, contact the publisher at info@courageousheartpress.com.

> These books are available at special discounts when purchased in quantity for use as premiums, promotions, fundraising and educational use. For inquiries and details, contact the publisher: info@courageousheartpress.com.

Paperback ISBN: 978-0-9969984-5-1
eBook ISBN: 978-0-9969984-6-8
LCCN: 2017938069

To Calla Mae Bumbalough Fleming (1908-2001)
A true mentor in the faith and a child of God

Contents

Author's Note ix
How to Use This Book.. xii
Setting the Scene... xv
Chapter 1: A Message from God 1
Chapter 2: Living in Times of Turbulence 7
Chapter 3: Living under Someone Else's Control 13
Chapter 4: Nurtured by God in a Foreign Land................... 19
Chapter 5: A Time to Stand and Act 25
Chapter 6: A Time to Praise 31
Chapter 7: Acknowledging and Honoring the Power of God 37
Chapter 8: King Nebuchadnezzar—Chosen by God................. 43
Chapter 9: God Reveals the Future to Nebuchadnezzar............ 49
Chapter 10: King Nebuchadnezzar Forgets God.................... 55
Chapter 11: Risking Their Lives to Honor God 61
Chapter 12: The King's Second Dream—God Tries Again........... 67
Chapter 13: God Gives Nebuchadnezzar Time 73
Chapter 14: King Belshazzar Sees the Writing on the Wall 79
Chapter 15: The Night Prophecy Was Fulfilled 85
Chapter 16: King Darius Regrets His Decree...................... 91
Chapter 17: God Saves Daniel from Death........................ 97
Chapter 18: Daniel Glimpses Eternity........................... 103
Chapter 19: Daniel's First Vision Interpreted.................... 109
Chapter 20: Daniel's Vision of the Ram and the Goat............. 115
Chapter 21: Daniel's Second Vision Explained 121
Chapter 22 : Daniel's Prayer 127
Chapter 23: The Seventy "Sevens" 133
Chapter 24: Daniel's Vision of a Man 139
Chapter 25: The Future Revealed to Daniel 145
Chapter 26: Difficult Times for God's People.................... 151
Chapter 27: The End Times—Great Changes to Come 157

Chapter 28: The End Times—God's Love and Care 163
Chapter 29: The Meaning of the Visions of Daniel 169
Chapter 30: Daniel—A Righteous and Wise Man of God 175
Chapter 31: Daniel—A Prophet of God 181
Resources. 187
For Further Study. 191
About the Author 193

Author's Note

If you've always thought the book of Daniel was too complex to understand, here's the good news: You don't have to understand everything in it in order to benefit from the many timeless and beautiful messages this book presents. After all, Daniel himself did not understand everything revealed to him, even when provided with a divine explanation.

What does shine through with clarity are the examples for living that Daniel and his friends left for us to discover. Even while living in the midst of chaos, change, and enduring life-threatening challenges, they chose to remain faithful to God. By surrendering their lives to God, they enjoyed a measure of peace, even in the direst of circumstances. We, too, can enjoy that same measure of peace today when we resolve to always serve God.

Why was this book written?

So how did someone who is not a Bible scholar come to write a book about Daniel? Several years ago, I began reading my Bible online. With this change came a bit of newness to the scriptures, and the words didn't seem quite as familiar. Even better, I could easily compare verses using multiple versions of the Bible. That's when this passage in Daniel Chapter 9 caught my attention:

> While I was speaking and praying, confessing my sin and the sin of my people Israel and making my request to the Lord my God for his holy hill—while I was still in prayer, Gabriel, the man I had seen in the earlier vision, came to me in swift flight about the time of the evening sacrifice. He instructed me and said to me, "Daniel, I have now come to give you

insight and understanding. As soon as you began to pray, a word went out, which I have come to tell you, for you are highly esteemed" (Daniel 9:20–23a NIV).

This stunning scripture triggered my *Aha!* moment in the study of the book of Daniel. Consider what is being said: Before Daniel had even finished praying, God not only responded to his prayer but also did so by means of the angel Gabriel! This is the same Gabriel who stands in the presence of God (Luke 1:19), the Gabriel who announced the upcoming births of John the Baptist and of Jesus. And you have to wonder if maybe Daniel, who was elderly by this time in his life, didn't get whiplash from the speed of God's response!

Why was God so attentive to Daniel? Because Daniel was "highly esteemed." Other versions use a variety of terms, such as greatly loved, highly respected, greatly treasured, greatly valued, or highly regarded. But the NIV's choice of the word, *esteemed*, seems to add even more dimension to the love God held for Daniel.

Think about the people whom you hold in high esteem. While you may love many people, you probably hold only a few in high esteem. For God to hold a mortal being in high esteem seems incredible. It speaks to the type of relationship that is possible for a human—for you and me—to have with God. It's a relationship definitely worth seeking.

For whom is this book written?

After the above scripture in Chapter 9 caught my eye, I began rereading the book of Daniel. This time, I decided to focus on what I *could* understand, because truthfully, I had allowed the parts I did *not* understand to overshadow my perception of the entire book. It's my supposition this has been the case for many other people as well.

So based upon my premise that others may have also shortchanged their study of the book of Daniel, I decided to purposely write this book to be understandable by a wide audience. Whether you've studied the Bible much or not at all, this book was written in the hope that you will be enriched by these lessons.

What about the meaning of Daniel's visions? While the Bible does explain some things, other things remain unclear. Remember that even Daniel failed to understand all of what he saw. Also, remember that when God wants to make things plain, He does. This scripture in Ecclesiastes 7:13 (NLT) comes to mind: **"Accept the way God does things, for who can straighten what he has made crooked?"**

My hope is that this book will help you seek out what you *can* understand from the book of Daniel, so you can benefit from the examples left us by Daniel and his friends. By resolving to serve God, no matter the circumstances, you, too, can find a measure of peace, even while living in a world of constant change. And may you aspire to live a life such that God may be able to say: *You are highly esteemed!*

> Don't worry about anything; instead, pray about everything. Tell God what you need, and thank him for all he has done. Then you will experience God's peace, which exceeds anything we can understand. His peace will guard your hearts and minds as you live in Christ Jesus.
> (Philippians 4:6–7 NLT)

How to Use This Book

This book may be used either for individual study or group study.

- For individual study, the thirty-one lessons plus the introduction could easily serve as a month of daily devotional studies. However, you could also extend your studies of this fascinating time in Jewish history much longer by using each lesson as a springboard for further research.
- For group study, two or more lessons could be covered each week, depending on the duration of your class. The outline below lists the scripture passages covered in each lesson to help the instructor create a syllabus for the class.

Life of Daniel & Friends

Lesson	Passage	Notes
Intro	n/a	
1	Jer. 25:1–14	
2	Dan. 1:1–7	
3	Dan. 1:1–7	
4	Dan. 1:8–21	
5	Dan. 2:1–19	
6	Dan. 2:17–23	
7	Dan. 2:24–45	
8	Dan. 2:28–45	
9	Dan. 2:31–49	
10	Dan. 3:1–7	

Life of Daniel & Friends Cont.

Lesson	Passage	Notes
11	Dan. 3:8–30	
12	Dan. 4:1–18	
13	Dan. 4:19–37	
14	Dan. 5:1–12	
15	Dan. 5:13–31	
16	Dan. 6:1–14	
17	Dan. 6:13–28	

Visions of Daniel

Lesson	Passage	Notes
18	Dan. 7:1–14	
19	Dan. 7:15–28	
20	Dan. 8:1–14	
21	Dan. 8:15–27	
22	Dan. 9:1–19	
23	Dan. 9:20–27	
24	Dan. 10:1–11:1	
25	Dan. 11:2–27	
26	Dan. 11:28–45	
27	Dan. 12:1–13	
28	Dan. 12:1–13	
29	Dan. 12:1–13	

Other Scriptures Referencing Daniel

Lesson	Passage	Notes
30	Ezek. 14:12–20; 28:1–3	
31	Matt. 24:1–21	

Note that the book of Daniel can be divided into two basic parts: Chapters 1-6 cover the life of Daniel and his friends, and Chapters 7-12 cover the visions or dreams of Daniel, with Daniel's prayer being in Chapter 9.

At the end of each lesson are three **Thoughts to Ponder** to help foster further personal study or to use for group discussions. The author's answers or thoughts on these Thoughts to Ponder will be available at the website, MarilynnHood.com/daniel. May this study of Daniel truly bless your life!

Setting the Scene

The happenings in the book of Daniel occurred during a momentous time for the Jewish people—their exile into Babylonian captivity. The coming of this tragedy, revealed to them well ahead of time, resulted in the total disruption of their lives. The brief review of Jewish history which follows will help set the scene for this unique book in the Bible.

After Moses led the Israelites (later referred to as Jews) out of Egyptian slavery, God sentenced them to wander in the wilderness for forty years until the generation of people who had originally come out of Egypt had died. Only Joshua and Caleb were spared this fate, due to their faith and confidence in God. It was Joshua who then oversaw the conquering of the Canaanites and the settling of the Israelites in the Promised Land.

For a number of years, as the twelve tribes of Israel spread out and established themselves in Canaan, a series of judges provided leadership. Although chosen by God, these people did not provide the strong, centralized leadership that Moses and Joshua had. Thwarted by the Philistines and other enemies, the people finally clamored for a king to lead them.

So, after more than three hundred years of judges, God chose Saul from the tribe of Benjamin as the first king of the Israelites. Unfortunately, Saul did not obey God's commands. In response, God took His favor from Saul and chose David, a shepherd boy from the tribe of Judah, to become king. God knew David to be "a man after His own heart" (1 Samuel 13:14 ESV) and promised to establish his throne forever. Indeed, Jesus Christ was born through David's lineage and sits on Heaven's throne today.

―――― 1 ――――

2 Kings, Chapters 24 and 25. These chapters provide the Biblical account of the events immediately leading up to the fall of Jerusalem and the ensuing events: the Babylonians looting the temple treasures, Nebuchadnezzar burning the temple, and the Jewish people being carried off into captivity.

Historical and Biblical Time Chart. This reference provides dates of occurrences from the call of Abraham in 2090 BC to beyond the time of Christ in the second century AD.

bit.ly/2IlFY6j

Israelite Kings Date Chart. This chart shows a listing of the kings from the first king, Saul, to the fall of Jerusalem and the Jewish exile into Babylonia.

bit.ly/2kUc5Jh

The Great Divorce: The Kingdom Divided. This writing gives a historical summary of the events leading to the divided kingdom and beyond.

bit.ly/2IlANmG

David's son, Solomon, built the magnificent temple of God in Jerusalem. As the third king, his reign in many ways represented the glory days of the kingdom of Israel. Because Solomon asked God for wisdom rather than wealth, God gave him that and everything else in absolute abundance. Unfortunately, he allowed his seven hundred wives and three hundred concubines to turn his heart toward foreign gods. As he was no longer solely devoted to God, God declared the kingdom would become divided.

After Solomon's death, the twelve tribes of Israel would no longer be united. God designated Jeroboam to lead the ten northern tribes, which became the kingdom of Israel. Rehoboam, Solomon's son, received only the remnant in the south, which became the kingdom of Judah. God preserved this portion in order to fulfill His promise to David that his lineage would continue.

For approximately the next two hundred years, the series of kings who ruled the northern kingdom of Israel were, for the most part, not committed to God. Some were particularly unfaithful, sinking deeply into pagan worship. Having turned their backs on God and His protection, the North fell to Assyria. The kings of the southern kingdom of Judah were a mixed lot, with some being notably good and others being notoriously bad. The South lasted more than one hundred years longer than did the North before falling to the Babylonians.

So it is here at this important juncture in history that the book of Daniel chronicles that fateful time of the Jewish exile into Babylonian captivity. God's chosen people had not held true to His commands and had been warned they would suffer this result. Many were killed during this time. Yet, because of His promise, God kept alive a remnant and preserved David's lineage, overseeing and protecting them even during this difficult time.[1]

Then Isaiah said to Hezekiah, "Hear the word of the Lord: The time will surely come when everything in your palace, and all that your predecessors have stored up until this day, will be carried off to Babylon. Nothing will be left, says the Lord. And some of your descendants, your own flesh and blood who will be born to you, will be taken away, and they will become eunuchs in the palace of the king of Babylon."

(2 Kings 10:16–18 NIV)

Ancient Jewish History: The Two Kingdoms. This historical summary provides an overview of Jewish history from Solomon to the Babylonian exile.

bit.ly/2lrZc6P

Timeline of the Babylonian Captivity. This timeline shows the estimated dates of events during this time period.

bit.ly/2lprl8j

The Destruction of Jerusalem: Overview of Nebuchadnezzar's Campaign Against Jerusalem. Read the summary and scroll down to view a map of the deportation.

bit.ly/2k4y5gw

Thoughts to Ponder

God's prophets clearly and loudly warned the Israelites they would be taken into Babylonian captivity. What, if anything, could the people and their kings have done to prevent or delay this event from occurring?

_____

_____

_____

_____

What did King Hezekiah do to change God's mind when he learned he was to die? (See 2 Kings 20 and Isaiah 38.) What example does this provide for God's people today?

_____

_____

_____

_____

Hezekiah was a good king (2 Kings 18:1–8), yet he was so human. After God granted him an extension on his life, what was his response when he learned the wealth of his kingdom, as well as his family members, would be carried to Babylon? (See 2 Kings 20:16–19.)

_____

_____

_____

_____

Chapter 1

A Message from God

Scripture reference: Jeremiah 25:1–14 (NIV)

(1) The word came to Jeremiah concerning all the people of Judah in the fourth year of Jehoiakim son of Josiah king of Judah, which was the first year of Nebuchadnezzar king of Babylon. (2) So Jeremiah the prophet said to all the people of Judah and to all those living in Jerusalem: (3) For twenty-three years—from the thirteenth year of Josiah son of Amon king of Judah until this very day—the word of the Lord has come to me and I have spoken to you again and again, but you have not listened.

(4) And though the Lord has sent all his servants the prophets to you again and again, you have not listened or paid any attention. (5) They said, "Turn now, each of you, from your evil ways and your evil practices, and you can stay in the land the Lord gave to you and your ancestors for ever and ever. (6) Do not follow other gods to serve and worship them; do not arouse my anger with what your hands have made. Then I will not harm you."

(7) "But you did not listen to me," declares the Lord, "and you have aroused my anger with what your hands have made, and you have brought harm to yourselves."

(8) Therefore the Lord Almighty says this: "Because you have not listened to my words, (9) I will summon all the peoples of the north and my servant Nebuchadnezzar king of Babylon," declares the Lord, "and I will bring them against this land and its inhabitants and against all the surrounding nations. I will completely destroy them and make them an object of horror and scorn,

---
1

Bible Timeline: Old Testament. This timeline provides approximate dates for the entire Old Testament.

bit.ly/2j8OMvl

The Rulers and Prophets of Daniel's Time. This picture timeline helps place the writings of the prophets, events, and kingdoms into a historical perspective.

bit.ly/2k5RvFp

and an everlasting ruin. (10) I will banish from them the sounds of joy and gladness, the voices of bride and bridegroom, the sound of millstones and the light of the lamp. (11) This whole country will become a desolate wasteland, and these nations will serve the king of Babylon seventy years.

(12) "But when the seventy years are fulfilled, I will punish the king of Babylon and his nation, the land of the Babylonians, for their guilt," declares the Lord, "and will make it desolate forever. (13) I will bring on that land all the things I have spoken against it, all that are written in this book and prophesied by Jeremiah against all the nations. (14) They themselves will be enslaved by many nations and great kings; I will repay them according to their deeds and the work of their hands."

What if you received a warning from God? Would you change your ways and dedicate your life to His service? No one today can say with certainty what they would have done if they had heard Jeremiah's message from God: "This whole country will become a desolate wasteland, and these nations will serve the king of Babylon seventy years" (Jeremiah 25:11 NIV). Thousands of years removed, we cannot fully understand the mindset of those who lived in such a different time and culture.

Regardless, the Israelites knew well ahead of time what was going to happen as a result of their unfaithfulness. More than one of God's prophets had warned them in no uncertain terms. Isaiah had issued a similar warning in Isaiah 39:5–7 decades earlier.[1] Like viewing a storm cloud brewing on the horizon, the Israelites could see this fateful string of events approaching.

The Babylonians ruthlessly attacked Jerusalem and defeated Jehoiakim, the king of Judah. During the course of several sieges, they virtually destroyed the city, setting fire to the temple of the Lord, the royal palace, and all the houses of Jerusalem. They burned every important building. The Babylonian army, under command of the imperial guard, tore down the walls around Jerusalem. They stripped the temple of its treasures and carried off sacred items which had been used in the worship of God.[2]

Little would remain of anything that had defined the Israelite nation; the life they had known was over. Those who weren't killed were carried off into Babylonian captivity. Only the poorest of the poor were left behind to tend the crops.[3]

Among the first wave of captives taken were Daniel, Hananiah, Mishael, and Azariah. Of royal lineage, these young men were likely teenagers or possibly pre-teens when led off to Babylon. Once there, these bright, capable, and handsome young men were specifically selected for three years of special training and grooming. Upon completion, they would then be ready to enter the king's service.

The book of Daniel opens with these four young Israelite men entering King Nebuchadnezzar's indoctrination program. No mention is made of their families. It's likely their parents and any siblings they may have had were either deceased or their whereabouts unknown. At any rate, they were completely uprooted from their lives of nobility in Jerusalem at a young age and evidently never returned to their homeland. Despite the loss of their family and the confusion of living in a new, pagan culture, Daniel, Hananiah, Mishael, and Azariah remained faithful to God.

Daniel—Esteemed by God

Because of Daniel's unwavering faith and his devotion to God, God held him in high regard. He was, in the words of the angel Gabriel, *highly esteemed* (Daniel 9:20–23 NIV). As such, Daniel was allowed to glimpse the future. His account of the historical events and the revelations he witnessed continues to resound through the ages, edifying generation after generation.

What would it take for you to become someone esteemed by God? Wouldn't that be the highest compliment you could ever receive? As you read through these lessons, observe Daniel's

---

— 2 —

The Babylonian Captivity with Map. Scroll through this site for an overview of this momentous time in Jewish history. Click through the links on the map to learn more.

bit.ly/2kW3OE8

Ancient Babylonia. Learn more about this powerful kingdom by scrolling through the site and clicking on the many links presented.

bit.ly/2kVUhNw

— 3 —

The Flight of the Prisoners. This painting provides the artist's interpretation of the arduous trek of the Jewish people into Babylonian captivity.

bit.ly/2eC1Rvz

character traits and consider what made him so special to God. Be inspired by the faith that he and his friends lived every day in their lives. Know that no matter what you face in your own life, whether it's an ordinary day or the fiery furnace, God will walk with you. Call upon Him, trust in Him, and most of all, set your sights on being someone esteemed by Him.

A hand touched me and set me trembling on my hands and knees. He said, "Daniel, you who are highly esteemed, consider carefully the words I am about to speak to you, and stand up, for I have now been sent to you." And when he said this to me, I stood up trembling. Then he continued, "Do not be afraid, Daniel. Since the first day that you set your mind to gain understanding and to humble yourself before your God, your words were heard, and I have come in response to them."

(Daniel 10:10–12 NIV)

Thoughts to Ponder

What did the Israelites do that made God so unhappy with them? (See Jeremiah 25:5–7.) How did they arouse God's anger with what their hands had made?

_____

_____

_____

_____

What types of "other gods" might people today be serving? How might "what your hands have made" cause problems for Christians today?

_____

_____

_____

_____

How did God use "the peoples of the north" and Nebuchadnezzar for His purposes? (As you study the book of Daniel, think on how God fulfilled this prophecy given in Jeremiah 25:9–14.)

_____

_____

_____

_____

Chapter 2

Living in Times of Turbulence

Scripture reference: Daniel 1:1–7 (HCSB)

(1) In the third year of the reign of Jehoiakim king of Judah, Nebuchadnezzar king of Babylon came to Jerusalem and laid siege to it. (2) The Lord handed Jehoiakim king of Judah over to him, along with some of the vessels from the house of God. Nebuchadnezzar carried them to the land of Babylon, to the house of his god, and put the vessels in the treasury of his god.

(3) The king ordered Ashpenaz, the chief of his court officials, to bring some of the Israelites from the royal family and from the nobility—(4) young men without any physical defect, good-looking, suitable for instruction in all wisdom, knowledgeable, perceptive, and capable of serving in the king's palace—and to teach them the Chaldean language and literature. (5) The king assigned them daily provisions from the royal food and from the wine that he drank. They were to be trained for three years, and at the end of that time, they were to serve in the king's court. (6) Among them, from the descendants of Judah, were Daniel, Hananiah, Mishael, and Azariah. (7) The chief official gave them other names: he gave the name Belteshazzar to Daniel, Shadrach to Hananiah, Meshach to Mishael, and Abednego to Azariah.

◇◇◇◇

---— 1 ——

Carchemish, and the Major Battle of 606 BCE. Read this article to learn more about the historical and pivotal battle fought at this ancient city.

bit.ly/2ISc46M

Emboldened by their defeat of the Assyrians in the great Battle of Carchemish, the Babylonians set their sights on Jerusalem.[1] What destruction the ruler, Nebuchadnezzar, wielded against the city! Stripping the temple, he carried its treasures off to Babylon. These items, which had been dedicated to the worship of the living God, would soon be debased and used in the service of the false Babylonian god. They would also play a part in the ruination of a future Babylonian king. (See Daniel Chapter 5, discussed in Lesson 14.)

As for the captives, can you imagine the great changes that must have suddenly and dramatically occurred in their lives? Seized from their homes, their country, and all that had been familiar to them, they were taken against their will to the distant land of Babylonia. The four young men introduced in this passage, Daniel, Hananiah, Mishael, and Azariah, had been born into nobility, but soon they would be destined to a life of servitude at the pleasure of King Nebuchadnezzar.

And what of their journey from Jerusalem to the city of Babylon? The direct distance would have been about five hundred miles—*if* they had cut across the desert; however, travelers in those times typically took a much longer route of about nine hundred miles, going north and then following the Euphrates River southeast. Scriptures state that when Ezra later made the return trip from Babylon to Jerusalem, it took him four months. (See Ezra 7:9.)

How did they travel? While it's possible some may have had access to donkeys or camels, it's quite likely most of the Jews walked. Every step took them farther from their homeland, and most never returned. If any of these exiles were among those allowed to come back years later to rebuild Jerusalem, they would have been elderly by that time. Their homes and the country they had known were now gone forever, a sad realization for the Jewish people as they trod the long road into the unknown.

When everything is changing around you, God is with you.

Writings later in the book of Daniel reveal the depths of the devotion these four young men introduced here—Daniel, Hananiah, Mishael, and Azariah—held toward God. They continued to believe in Him and serve Him, even when forced to live in a foreign land where false gods were worshipped. They took their one true and living God with them in their hearts, knowing that, with Him, they could face whatever lay ahead.

Yes, God allowed the Jewish people to be subjected to seventy years of Babylonian captivity, *but He never turned away from the individuals who remained His faithful servants.* He went with them into this foreign land, watching over them and protecting them, even placing some in positions of power and authority.

Today, God continues to walk alongside His faithful, just as he did with Daniel, Hananiah, Mishael, and Azariah. When your world shifts and changes and perhaps crashes around you, remember how God cared for and delivered His faithful servants of old. God strengthened them, protected them, and helped them bear their burdens, even as they lived as captives in a foreign land. Though their very lives were severely threatened at times, their faithfulness gave them inner peace. Their belief in God did not waver, and He faithfully saw them through the dangers and treachery they faced.

Take heart in knowing that the same God is right here today. He cares for His faithful now, just as He did Daniel and his friends so long ago.

Every good and perfect gift is from above, coming down from the Father of the heavenly lights, who does not change like shifting shadows.
(James 1:17 NIV)

Thoughts to Ponder

Compare the account of what happened here with what had been prophesied years before. (Reread 2 Kings 20:16–18 or Isaiah 39:5–7.) Do you think these young men were among the descendants referred to in this prophecy?

_____

_____

_____

_____

Even though God was unhappy with the nation, He did not blanketly condemn every person. List some of the many ways God showed His favor to these four young men.

_____

_____

_____

_____

God's people are never "lost in the crowd" in God's eyes. Consider the teachings in the New Testament, particularly the parables of Jesus. How did Jesus emphasize the importance of each individual?

_____

_____

_____

_____

Chapter 3

Living under Someone Else's Control

Scripture reference: Daniel 1:1–7 (MSG)

(This is the same passage as in Lesson 2, but we're looking at a different version to gain a broader perspective.)

(1–2) It was the third year of King Jehoiakim's reign in Judah when King Nebuchadnezzar of Babylon declared war on Jerusalem and besieged the city. The Master handed King Jehoiakim of Judah over to him, along with some of the furnishings from the Temple of God. Nebuchadnezzar took king and furnishings to the country of Babylon, the ancient Shinar. He put the furnishings in the sacred treasury.

(3–5) The king told Ashpenaz, head of the palace staff, to get some Israelites from the royal family and nobility—young men who were healthy and handsome, intelligent and well-educated, good prospects for leadership positions in the government, perfect specimens!—and indoctrinate them in the Babylonian language and the lore of magic and fortunetelling. The king then ordered that they be served from the same menu as the royal table—the best food, the finest wine. After three years of training they would be given positions in the king's court.

(6–7) Four young men from Judah—Daniel, Hananiah, Mishael, and Azariah—were among those selected. The head of the palace staff gave them Babylonian names: Daniel was named Belteshazzar, Hananiah was named Shadrach, Mishael was named Meshach, Azariah was named Abednego.

1

Ancient tablets reveal life of Jews in Nebuchadnezzar's Babylon. This article, complete with a short video and slides, allows a glimpse of what daily life was like for the Jews during their exile.

reut.rs/2kTbyXs

◇◇◇◇

Forced from their Promised Land, the Jews who were taken into exile would now live as strangers in a foreign land. Great challenges lay before them, as will clearly be seen in later chapters. While the discovery of ancient tablets[1] indicate they did not suffer to the degree their ancestors had during Egyptian slavery, Ezra's writings refer to them as being slaves in bondage: "… so our God gives light to our eyes and a little relief in our bondage. Though we are slaves, our God has not forsaken us in our bondage. He has shown us kindness in the sight of the kings of Persia …" (Ezra 9:8b–9a NIV).

Especially impacted were the lives of the four young men introduced in this passage, Daniel, Hananiah, Mishael, and Azariah. The king sought certain of the Jewish nobility, the "cream of the crop," to assume leadership positions within his government. So, after enduring the long journey from Jerusalem to Babylon, these four young men were among those chosen to begin a three-year course of training.

Think for a moment what this "training" meant: These young men were to be indoctrinated with all things Babylonian. They were to learn the language along with the history and traditions of the culture. They were expected to eat different foods from what they were accustomed. In fact, some scholars believe they could have been emasculated, or made eunuchs. What is the reasoning behind this assumption? Recall for a moment the words of Isaiah's prophecy presented earlier:

> Then Isaiah said to Hezekiah, "Hear the word of the Lord: The time will surely come when everything in your palace, and all that your predecessors have stored up until this day, will be carried off to Babylon. Nothing will be left, says the Lord. And some of your descendants, your own flesh and blood who will be born to you, will be taken away, and they will become eunuchs in the palace of the king of Babylon." (2 Kings 20:16–18 NIV)

Whether Isaiah was speaking in general terms or about specific people is not clear. Regardless, these young men had been taken from their families, their homes, their country, their culture and their customs. Now they were to be reprogrammed for the king's service.

Consider the extent to which Nebuchadnezzar sought to change them: Their physical bodies with the food and wine they were given to consume, their minds with the new language and culture they were to absorb, and most importantly, their spiritual being with the training in "the lore of magic and fortunetelling." (The Babylonians believed in supernatural forces and the existence of other gods.) In effect, Nebuchadnezzar sought to change their entire being.

Then, to complete the process of taking total control and dominating these young men's lives, the chief official changed their names. Think for a moment: Your name is your personal identifier. It's what you've been called since birth, a gift bestowed upon you by your parents. It sets you apart from everyone else. So for these young men, even their personal identity was to be taken from them.

When everything is taken from you, God is with you.

Yes, Nebuchadnezzar sought to control every aspect of these young men's lives. Even so, they understood the personal power which lay within them. Using their logic and reasoning skills, they swayed Ashpenaz, the official in charge, to allow them to eat healthier foods and drink water. Knowing their belief in God could not be taken from them, they drew upon their unwavering faith time and again to carry them through the difficulties they faced while living in Babylonian captivity.

In short, these young men realized that their minds were their most valuable and powerful possession. It's the same today. Even when your world changes around you and you feel as if the rug has been pulled out from under your feet, you still have the power to control your mind. Others may seek to control every aspect of your lives, yet your belief in God is something that cannot be taken from you—unless you allow it.

Feed your mind with good things. Nurture your spiritual development with knowledge of the scriptures. Remember that your faith in God will always remain under your control, if you so choose.

Do not be anxious about anything, but in every situation, by prayer and petition, with thanksgiving, present your requests to God. And the peace of God, which transcends all understanding, will guard your hearts and your minds in Christ Jesus.
(Philippians 4:6–7 NIV)

Thoughts to Ponder

What do you think was Nebuchadnezzar's purpose in seeking to indoctrinate God's people? Why did he select the "cream of the crop?"

_____

_____

_____

_____

How did these young men use their minds to prevent the total indoctrination that Nebuchadnezzar sought?

_____

_____

_____

_____

How can you use your mind today when others seek to influence and control you? How can you bolster your resolve to serve God and always do the right thing?

_____

_____

_____

_____

Chapter 4

Nurtured by God in a Foreign Land

Scripture reference: Daniel 1:8–21 (HCSB)

(8) Daniel determined that he would not defile himself with the king's food or with the wine he drank. So he asked permission from the chief official not to defile himself. (9) God had granted Daniel favor and compassion from the chief official, (10) yet he said to Daniel, "My lord the king assigned your food and drink. I'm afraid of what would happen if he saw your faces looking thinner than those of the other young men your age. You would endanger my life with the king."

(11) So Daniel said to the guard whom the chief official had assigned to Daniel, Hananiah, Mishael, and Azariah, (12) "Please test your servants for 10 days. Let us be given vegetables to eat and water to drink. (13) Then examine our appearance and the appearance of the young men who are eating the king's food, and deal with your servants based on what you see." (14) He agreed with them about this and tested them for 10 days. (15) At the end of 10 days they looked better and healthier than all the young men who were eating the king's food. (16) So the guard continued to remove their food and the wine they were to drink and gave them vegetables.

(17) God gave these four young men knowledge and understanding in every kind of literature and wisdom. Daniel also understood visions and dreams of every kind. (18) At the end of the time that the king had said to present them,

the chief official presented them to Nebuchadnezzar. **(19)** The king interviewed them, and among all of them, no one was found equal to Daniel, Hananiah, Mishael, and Azariah. So they began to serve in the king's court. **(20)** In every matter of wisdom and understanding that the king consulted them about, he found them 10 times better than all the diviner-priests and mediums in his entire kingdom. **(21)** Daniel remained there until the first year of King Cyrus.

How do you maintain control of your life when someone else calls the shots? Acting with respect, using logic, and leaning on God were the tools these young men used to retain at least a measure of control in their lives.

Review for a moment all that had been taken from Daniel and his friends—physically, mentally, and spiritually—as they were forced into Babylonian captivity:

- Their tranquility—It was a time of wars and battles, with King Nebuchadnezzar overcoming and destroying Jerusalem.
- Their homes and families—Taken as captives to the foreign country of Babylonia, they probably walked for months to get there. There is no record that any of them ever returned to their homeland or were reunited with their families.
- Their positions in society—As members of the royal family, they had enjoyed a life of nobility. Now, they served at the pleasure of a foreign king.
- Their sacred place of worship—Central to Jewish worship, the temple in Jerusalem had been chosen by God for His dwelling place. King Nebuchadnezzar defiled this most holy place, carrying off many of the items dedicated for worshipping God to use for his own pleasure.
- Their names—Replacing their personal identity from birth, the chief official assigned them new names. While the

meaning behind their Hebrew names had all honored God, their new names associated them with false pagan gods. Certainly, this served as a direct attempt to change them at the core of their being.[1]

- Their heritage and culture—Just as the homeland they left behind would never be the same, neither would their traditions or their day-to-day culture. Going forward, they were to be indoctrinated with all things Babylonian, including learning the language.
- Their diet—God had given instructions to the Jewish people concerning the kinds of foods they could eat and how to prepare them. Had they eaten what the king provided for them, their physical health might have suffered, and they would likely have violated God's dietary laws as well.
- Their clothes—Although not specifically mentioned, wearing clothing supplied by King Nebuchadnezzar would have altered their outward appearance and served to constantly remind them of their new identity.

Keep God in your heart, and He will nurture you.

While every aspect of their lives appeared to be under the control of someone else, these young men's devotion to God remained intact in their hearts and minds. God nurtured them from within and supplied them with strength and courage, as well as with knowledge and understanding.

God also softened the heart of their guard so that he treated them favorably. When Daniel had the courage to speak up and ask that they be given different food, the guard listened to him and carefully considered his request. Rather than making a demand of the guard, Daniel spoke with tact and reasoned with him.

He also presented the guard with a logical alternative: to examine their appearance after a ten-day trial and then make his decision. That way, the guard could remedy the situation if he

---

1

Behind the Name. Look up the meaning of names on this site.

behindthename.com

The Name Changes. This lecture by Floyd Hitchcock explains the meaning of both the Jewish and Babylonian names of Daniel and his friends.

bit.ly/2li6GfB

felt it necessary. Daniel wisely showed the guard how he could comply with his request without jeopardizing either his job or his life.

When you face difficult situations, remember how Daniel and his friends used logic and tact—and totally relied upon God. Ask God to give you wisdom in the words you choose and the actions you take. Know that God will remain in your heart and mind, no matter the conditions you face, if you will allow Him. Let His love be like a well of living water within you, and He will supply and sustain you. Draw strength from Him and ask that He constantly guide you—in thought, in word, and in deed.

"... but whoever drinks the water I give them will never thirst. Indeed, the water I give them will become in them a spring of water welling up to eternal life."

(John 4:14 NIV)

Thoughts to Ponder

How did Daniel, even though he was in a position of servitude, gain control of this situation and bring about the outcome he desired?

_____

_____

_____

_____

Daniel, who was a young person at this time, showed great wisdom here and throughout the rest of his life. Consider wisdom and its great value. (Read and dwell on Proverbs 4, Proverbs 8, and other scriptures on wisdom.) In what ways can you acquire godly wisdom?

_____

_____

_____

_____

Does God bestow wisdom on His people today? (See James 1:5.) Consider the value of wisdom in your life.

_____

_____

_____

_____

Chapter 5

A Time to Stand and Act

Scripture reference: Daniel 2:1–19 (HCSB)

(1) In the second year of his reign, Nebuchadnezzar had dreams that troubled him, and sleep deserted him. **(2)** So the king gave orders to summon the diviner-priests, mediums, sorcerers, and Chaldeans to tell the king his dreams. When they came and stood before the king, **(3)** he said to them, "I have had a dream and am anxious to understand it."

(4) The Chaldeans spoke to the king (Aramaic begins here): "May the king live forever. Tell your servants the dream, and we will give the interpretation."

(5) The king replied to the Chaldeans, "My word is final: If you don't tell me the dream and its interpretation, you will be torn limb from limb, and your houses will be made a garbage dump. **(6)** But if you make the dream and its interpretation known to me, you'll receive gifts, a reward, and great honor from me. So make the dream and its interpretation known to me."

(7) They answered a second time, "May the king tell the dream to his servants, and we will give the interpretation."

(8) The king replied, "I know for certain you are trying to gain some time, because you see that my word is final. **(9)** If you don't tell me the dream, there is one decree for you. You have conspired to tell me something false or fraudulent until the situation changes. So tell me the dream and I will know you can give me its interpretation."

(10) The Chaldeans answered the king, "No one on earth can make known what the king requests. Consequently, no king, however great and powerful, has ever asked anything like this of any diviner-priest, medium, or Chaldean. **(11)** What the king is asking is so difficult that no one can make it known to him except the gods, whose dwelling is not with mortals." **(12)** Because of this, the king became violently angry and gave orders to destroy all the wise men of Babylon. **(13)** The decree was issued that the wise men were to be executed, and they searched for Daniel and his friends, to execute them.

(14) Then Daniel responded with tact and discretion to Arioch, the commander of the king's guard, who had gone out to execute the wise men of Babylon. **(15)** He asked Arioch, the king's officer, "Why is the decree from the king so harsh?" Then Arioch explained the situation to Daniel. **(16)** So Daniel went and asked the king to give him some time, so that he could give the king the interpretation.

(17) Then Daniel went to his house and told his friends Hananiah, Mishael, and Azariah about the matter, **(18)** urging them to ask the God of heaven for mercy concerning this mystery, so Daniel and his friends would not be killed with the rest of Babylon's wise men. **(19)** The mystery was then revealed to Daniel in a vision at night, and Daniel praised the God of heaven ….

Have you ever had a dream that seemed so real, when you awoke you were still immersed in it? King Nebuchadnezzar had such a dream, and it disturbed him. He felt certain this particular dream held great significance, but he didn't know what it could be. He called upon the magicians, enchanters, sorcerers, astrologers and the Chaldeans—all those who were supposedly gifted with supernatural insight—to interpret his dream.

As a conqueror of nations, King Nebuchadnezzar was both powerful and shrewd. Rather than reveal his dream to these "wise" men, he demanded they tell him what his dream had been. He put them to the supreme test to determine if they really had extraordinary abilities. (Having been associated with them, it's possible he had his doubts.) This time, the king refused to be deceived—his dream felt too important to leave its interpretation to liars.

When the wise men heard the king's unusual request, they were shocked. What Nebuchadnezzar had demanded was too difficult. "No one can reveal it to the king except the gods," they responded, "and they do not live among humans" (Daniel 2:11 NIV). With this statement, they essentially admitted they lacked divine guidance.

Even when things seem hopeless, God will help you stand and take action.

Realizing the wise men were not actually gifted, the king became enraged. He commanded that *every* wise man in the country, not just those he had summoned, be killed! This included Daniel and his friends.

When Arioch, the commander of the king's guard, found Daniel and told him the king had ordered his execution, Daniel again replied with wisdom and tact. How difficult this must have been for him with his life on the line! Yet Daniel knew he could trust in God, no matter what might occur. This faith helped him stand and take action rather than buckle at the knees and collapse in fear.

With nothing to lose and his life to save, Daniel acted with courage. Rather than plead with Arioch, who was only the messenger, he went to the source of the order. He appealed directly to the king for time to interpret the dream.

Knowing that his own life and those of many others depended upon God, Daniel handed Him his dilemma. He called upon his friends to pray as well. Truthfully, Daniel knew that whether he lived or whether he died, he could be at peace—he belonged to the Almighty. This inner peace and his assurance of God's constant care helped Daniel to stand, take action, and behave rationally even while his life hung in the balance.

What if, out of the blue, you were told you were to be executed—not because of a crime you had committed, but because you were considered part of a class of people? How would you handle such a desperate situation? Fear or rage might be your initial response, but those emotions won't bring peace to your life. Only God can do that, regardless of the circumstances. Even if your life isn't on the line, you can always choose to turn to the Almighty—the Creator of the universe—for help, strength, courage, and peace.

Remember that today God continues to help the faithful to stand and gives them the courage to act, even when faced with their greatest fears. Know that no matter what the adversity, in life or in death, God cares for His children and will see them through.

Humble yourselves, therefore, under God's mighty hand, that he may lift you up in due time. Cast all your anxiety on him because he cares for you.

(I Peter 5:6–7 NIV)

Thoughts to Ponder

What would be the natural reaction for most people if they were unexpectedly told they were to be executed?

_____

_____

_____

_____

Have you ever found yourself in a life-or-death situation? How did you handle it? How would you hope to handle a dire situation, should one arise in the future?

_____

_____

_____

_____

Can you, like the apostle Paul, truly say, "For to me, to live is Christ and to die is gain" (Philippians 1:21 NIV)? What advice does he give in the verses that follow? (See Philippians 1:27–30.)

_____

_____

_____

_____

Chapter 6

A Time to Praise

Scripture reference: Daniel 2:17–23 (NASB)

(17) Then Daniel went to his house and informed his friends, Hananiah, Mishael and Azariah, about the matter, **(18)** so that they might request compassion from the God of heaven concerning this mystery, so that Daniel and his friends would not be destroyed with the rest of the wise men of Babylon. **(19)** Then the mystery was revealed to Daniel in a night vision. Then Daniel blessed the God of heaven; **(20)** Daniel said,

> "Let the name of God be blessed forever and ever,
> For wisdom and power belong to Him.

(21)   "It is He who changes the times and the epochs;
> He removes kings and establishes kings;
> He gives wisdom to wise men
> And knowledge to men of understanding.

(22)   "It is He who reveals the profound and hidden things;
> He knows what is in the darkness,
> And the light dwells with Him.

(23)   "To You, O God of my fathers, I give thanks and praise,
> For You have given me wisdom and power;
> Even now You have made known to me what we requested of You,
> For You have made known to us the king's matter."

◇◇◇◇

Have you ever been faced with a situation so desperate that your life hung in the balance? Daniel and his friends certainly did, and they knew that only God's divine intervention could save them. Together, they turned to the Almighty in prayer and asked for His help.

What relief Daniel and his friends must have felt when God revealed the mystery of King Nebuchadnezzar's dream to him! Because of this, all their lives were spared. With a grateful heart, Daniel offered this song of praise in Daniel 2:20–23. (Take time to read it again and dwell upon its beauty and meaning.)

But think for a moment—what if God had *not* granted their request? Would it have meant that God was not listening? No, the Bible states many times that God hears the prayers of the righteous (Proverbs 15:29, Psalm 34:15). Sometimes, however, what the righteous ask for is not part of God's plan.

Consider the Apostle Paul and how God denied his request to remove his "thorn in the flesh" (2 Corinthians 12:7–9 NIV). Or consider Jesus and how earnestly He prayed in the Garden of Gethsemane that the cup be taken from Him. God always hears, but He doesn't always say yes. Jesus understood this when He ended His prayer with, "… not as I will, but as you will" (Matthew 26:39 ESV).

When things go well for you, remember to thank and praise God.

It's so easy to call out to God when in distress. Yet, when things work out, when you receive relief, do you remember to stop and give thanks for God's deliverance? Sometimes, after being so wrapped up, first in the pressing situation and then with trying to move on afterward, it's easy to forget to make time for praise.

Daniel's actions and words provide a strong example for Christians today. He did what he could from a practical standpoint—he begged the king for time. It's likely the king responded favorably because he already knew Daniel to be an exceptional person. A good reputation is always a valuable asset.

Next, Daniel called upon his close friends to lend their support and beg for God's mercy and wisdom. Always remember to ask others to pray for you and with you as well. Today's technology often allows almost instant access to others. Understand how important your prayer requests are and have the courage to reach out and involve others. Remember Jesus's words in Matthew 18:20 (KJV), "For where two or three are gathered together in my name, there am I in the midst of them." What power Christians have!

Finally, after being granted his request, Daniel praised God with all his heart. He gave recognition to God's mighty power and wisdom. He thanked God for revealing the King's dream to him. His words were eloquent and beautifully spoken, but most importantly, they came from his heart.

Always remember to give thanks to God, no matter how a situation may turn out. You may not understand why things happen as they do, but trust in the Lord no matter what. Your words of praise may not flow as beautifully as Daniel's, but that's okay. God will still appreciate your sincere utterances, even the most clumsily worded. And most importantly, expressing words of praise will bring you closer to God. Dwell for a moment on the following words of joy and praise, penned so long ago.

Shout for joy to the Lord, all the earth.

Worship the Lord with gladness;
come before him with joyful songs.

Know that the Lord is God.
It is he who made us, and we are his;
we are his people, the sheep of his pasture.

Enter his gates with thanksgiving
and his courts with praise;
give thanks to him and praise his name.

For the Lord is good and his love endures forever;
his faithfulness continues through all generations.
(Psalm 100 NIV)

Thoughts to Ponder

How did King Nebuchadnezzar's refusal to reveal the contents of his dream work to Daniel's ultimate advantage? Has adversity ever worked to your advantage?

_____

_____

_____

_____

Consider the roller coaster ride of emotions that Daniel had to handle during this relatively short period of time, going from a regular day to facing his execution to his ultimate delivery. How would these events have impacted you?

_____

_____

_____

_____

If God had chosen <u>not</u> to reveal King Nebuchadnezzar's dream to Daniel, what do you think Daniel's response would have been? What would your response have been?

_____

_____

_____

_____

Chapter 7

Acknowledging and Honoring the Power of God

Scripture reference: Daniel 2:24–45 (HCSB)

(24) Therefore Daniel went to Arioch, whom the king had assigned to destroy the wise men of Babylon. He came and said to him, "Don't kill the wise men of Babylon! Bring me before the king, and I will give him the interpretation."

(25) Then Arioch quickly brought Daniel before the king and said to him, "I have found a man among the Judean exiles who can let the king know the interpretation."

(26) The king said in reply to Daniel, whose name was Belteshazzar, "Are you able to tell me the dream I had and its interpretation?"

(27) Daniel answered the king: "No wise man, medium, diviner-priest, or astrologer is able to make known to the king the mystery he asked about. (28) But there is a God in heaven who reveals mysteries, and He has let King Nebuchadnezzar know what will happen in the last days. Your dream and the visions that came into your mind as you lay in bed were these: (29) Your Majesty, while you were in your bed, thoughts came to your mind about what will happen in the future. The revealer of mysteries has let you know what will happen. (30) As for me, this mystery has been revealed to me, not because I have more wisdom than anyone living, but in order that the interpretation might be made known to the king, and that you may understand the thoughts of your mind.

(31) "My king, as you were watching, a colossal statue appeared. That statue, tall and dazzling, was standing in front of you, and its appearance was terrifying. (32) The head of the statue was pure gold, its chest and arms were silver, its stomach and thighs were bronze, (33) its legs were iron, and its feet were partly iron and partly fired clay. (34) As you were watching, a stone broke off without a hand touching it, struck the statue on its feet of iron and fired clay, and crushed them. (35) Then the iron, the fired clay, the bronze, the silver, and the gold were shattered and became like chaff from the summer threshing floors. The wind carried them away, and not a trace of them could be found. But the stone that struck the statue became a great mountain and filled the whole earth.

(36) "This was the dream; now we will tell the king its interpretation. (37) Your Majesty, you are king of kings. The God of heaven has given you sovereignty, power, strength, and glory. (38) Wherever people live—or wild animals, or birds of the air—He has handed them over to you and made you ruler over them all. You are the head of gold.

(39) "After you, there will arise another kingdom, inferior to yours, and then another, a third kingdom, of bronze, which will rule the whole earth. (40) A fourth kingdom will be as strong as iron; for iron crushes and shatters everything, and like iron that smashes, it will crush and smash all the others. (41) You saw the feet and toes, partly of a potter's fired clay and partly of iron—it will be a divided kingdom, though some of the strength of iron will be in it. You saw the iron mixed with clay, (42) and that the toes of the feet were partly iron and partly fired clay—part of the kingdom will be strong, and part will be brittle. (43) You saw the iron mixed with clay—the peoples will mix with one another but will not hold together, just as iron does not mix with fired clay.

(44) "In the days of those kings, the God of heaven will set up a kingdom that will never be destroyed, and this kingdom will not be left to another people. It will crush all these kingdoms and bring them to an end, but will itself endure forever. (45) You saw a stone break

off from the mountain without a hand touching it, and it crushed the iron, bronze, fired clay, silver, and gold. The great God has told the king what will happen in the future. The dream is true, and its interpretation certain."

King Nebuchadnezzar knew that his dream was no ordinary dream. Its disturbing contents compelled him to take action, to seek someone who could explain its meaning to him. All the wise men in the kingdom knew the accurate interpretation of the king's dream was of grave importance to him—their lives were at risk!

Imagine everyone's relief when Daniel stepped forward. With courage and confidence he asked for an audience with the king. He knew his life was at stake, too, but he also knew God had given him the interpretation that Nebuchadnezzar so desperately sought.

Always remember to give God the glory.

It would have been so easy for Daniel to take the credit for providing the dream's interpretation. After all, God had chosen to reveal it to him. Yet before he ever began, Daniel acknowledged that his message was from God, not from him.

Daniel also told the king the dream's meaning had been revealed to him—not because he had more wisdom than anyone else alive—but because God wanted the king to understand this message. He made it clear that he was simply the messenger, and not the originator, of the dream's interpretation.

If anyone had reason to exalt himself, or at least give himself some amount of credit, surely it would have been Daniel. Exceptional in so many ways, Daniel was one of the most highly educated people in Babylon—and probably in the world—at that time.

Yet, Daniel was truly humble. He worshipped God, listened to God, and remembered to praise and honor Him. The way Daniel lived his life has provided an example for untold thousands through the ages and continues to inspire even today.

Whatever your position in life, whether low or high, whether educated and powerful or not, remember the humility with which Daniel lived his life. Seek to live your life in a way that will inspire others, perhaps even future generations whom you will never meet. Live a life that will bring glory to God's name.

"Submit yourselves, then, to God. Resist the devil, and he will flee from you. Come near to God and he will come near to you …. Humble yourselves before the Lord, and he will lift you up."
(James 4:7–8, 10 NIV)

Thoughts to Ponder

Arioch had been appointed by Nebuchadnezzar as the executioner of the wise men. Had he not fulfilled his job as ordered, his own life would have been on the line. Why do you think he responded so favorably to Daniel?

_____

_____

_____

_____

How do you think Daniel felt standing before the King, whose temper was so volatile that he had ordered death for all the wise men? How would you feel standing before someone who had ordered your death?

_____

_____

_____

_____

God could have spoken clearly and directly to Nebuchadnezzar. Why do you think He chose to use a dream that needed to be interpreted by someone else? How many other people's lives were impacted because of the way God chose to communicate?

_____

_____

_____

_____

Chapter 8

King Nebuchadnezzar— Chosen by God

Scripture reference: Daniel 2:28–45 (NLT)

(This is the same passage as in Lesson 7, but we're looking at a different version to gain a broader perspective.)

(28) "But there is a God in heaven who reveals secrets, and he has shown King Nebuchadnezzar what will happen in the future. Now I will tell you your dream and the visions you saw as you lay on your bed. **(29)** While Your Majesty was sleeping, you dreamed about coming events. He who reveals secrets has shown you what is going to happen. **(30)** And it is not because I am wiser than anyone else that I know the secret of your dream, but because God wants you to understand what was in your heart.

(31) "In your vision, Your Majesty, you saw standing before you a huge, shining statue of a man. It was a frightening sight. **(32)** The head of the statue was made of fine gold. Its chest and arms were silver, its belly and thighs were bronze, **(33)** its legs were iron, and its feet were a combination of iron and baked clay. **(34)** As you watched, a rock was cut from a mountain, but not by human hands. It struck the feet of iron and clay, smashing them to bits. **(35)** The whole statue was crushed into small pieces of iron, clay, bronze, silver, and gold. Then the wind blew them away without a trace, like chaff on a threshing floor. But the rock that knocked the statue down became a great mountain that covered the whole earth.

(36) "That was the dream. Now we will tell the king what it means. **(37)** Your Majesty, you are the greatest of kings. The God of heaven has given you sovereignty, power, strength, and honor. **(38)** He has made you the ruler over all the inhabited world and has put even the wild animals and birds under your control. You are the head of gold.

(39) "But after your kingdom comes to an end, another kingdom, inferior to yours, will rise to take your place. After that kingdom has fallen, yet a third kingdom, represented by bronze, will rise to rule the world. **(40)** Following that kingdom, there will be a fourth one, as strong as iron. That kingdom will smash and crush all previous empires, just as iron smashes and crushes everything it strikes. **(41)** The feet and toes you saw were a combination of iron and baked clay, showing that this kingdom will be divided. Like iron mixed with clay, it will have some of the strength of iron. **(42)** But while some parts of it will be as strong as iron, other parts will be as weak as clay. **(43)** This mixture of iron and clay also shows that these kingdoms will try to strengthen themselves by forming alliances with each other through intermarriage. But they will not hold together, just as iron and clay do not mix.

(44) "During the reigns of those kings, the God of heaven will set up a kingdom that will never be destroyed or conquered. It will crush all these kingdoms into nothingness, and it will stand forever. **(45)** That is the meaning of the rock cut from the mountain, though not by human hands, that crushed to pieces the statue of iron, bronze, clay, silver, and gold. The great God was showing the king what will happen in the future. The dream is true, and its meaning is certain."

Nebuchadnezzar was not an Israelite. He was not from the lineage of Jacob, God's chosen people. Yet God selected him, the king of an enemy nation, to carry out His will. This time, however, God's will was to punish His people for their disobedience.

The prophet Jeremiah foretold God's plan and the part Nebuchadnezzar was to play in Jeremiah 25. In fact, Jeremiah proclaimed it publicly and must have been very vocal about his message from God. (Refer back to Lesson 1.) The scriptures say that he spoke to "all the people of Judah and to all those living in Jerusalem" (Jeremiah 25:2 NIV). Jerusalem, of course, was special. It was the place God had chosen for the temple to be built and for His Name to dwell (2 Chronicles 6:4–11). Jeremiah made sure the inhabitants of Jerusalem heard his message.

Why was God angry with His people? They had adopted evil ways and evil practices. They had turned from worshipping God and were serving false gods. In fact, they were worshipping things they had made with their own hands (Jeremiah 25: 5–6). These false gods were useless and powerless, whereas God Almighty had delivered them from Egyptian slavery. He had proven His power repeatedly by rescuing them, providing for them, and protecting them. He had given them their own land and made them a great people.

God can choose anyone to make Himself known.

After sending His prophets again and again to warn the people and to urge them to turn from evil, God had finally had enough. He appointed Nebuchadnezzar as His servant to destroy their land, the temple, and all they held dear. Even the nations surrounding the Israelite people would be destroyed. Those who were "lucky" enough to survive the siege could look forward to seventy years of captivity in the land of Babylonia.

Did Nebuchadnezzar know God had chosen him and put him in this position of power? Until this dream, he probably didn't. It's likely he thought his greatness was due to his own efforts. But in this dream, Daniel revealed to the king that it was God who had given him his strength and made him the most powerful ruler on earth.

The statue in the dream represented various kingdoms. Enormous in size and dazzling with brilliance, this statue was awesome to behold. And there was Nebuchadnezzar at the head of this great statue! What an honor, not only that God had placed him in this position, but also that this head was pure gold. Truly, the Babylonian empire represented a golden era in time that was superior in many ways to those which were to follow.

Yes, God chose Nebuchadnezzar, but He has also chosen you. Where has God placed you? Maybe not in such an illustrious and exalted position as the king of Babylonia and ruler of much of the known world, but you play just as important a role in God's plan. The talents you possess are uniquely yours. Remember that God has given them to you and only to you. Recognize their beauty, consider their great value, and commit to using, always to His glory, the precious gifts which God has given you.

"You are the light of the world. A town built on a hill cannot be hidden. Neither do people light a lamp and put it under a bowl. Instead they put it on its stand, and it gives light to everyone in the house. In the same way, let your light shine before others, that they may see your good deeds and glorify your Father in heaven."

(Matthew 5:14–16 NIV)

Thoughts to Ponder

Daniel explained to Nebuchadnezzar that it was God who had placed him in his position of power. What other great ruler (who was not an Israelite) did God place in power over His people? (See Romans 9:16–18 and Exodus 9:13–18.)

_____

_____

_____

_____

What was God's purpose in placing oppressive rulers over His people?

_____

_____

_____

_____

Why would God allow the destruction of what had been created for His Name? What value were these earthly items to God, the Creator of the universe?

_____

_____

_____

_____

Chapter 9

God Reveals the Future to Nebuchadnezzar

Scripture reference: Daniel 2:31–49 (NASB)

(31) "You, O king, were looking and behold, there was a single great statue; that statue, which was large and of extraordinary splendor, was standing in front of you, and its appearance was awesome. **(32)** The head of that statue *was made* of fine gold, its breast and its arms of silver, its belly and its thighs of bronze, **(33)** its legs of iron, its feet partly of iron and partly of clay. **(34)** You continued looking until a stone was cut out without hands, and it struck the statue on its feet of iron and clay and crushed them. **(35)** Then the iron, the clay, the bronze, the silver and the gold were crushed all at the same time and became like chaff from the summer threshing floors; and the wind carried them away so that not a trace of them was found. But the stone that struck the statue became a great mountain and filled the whole earth.

(36) "This *was* the dream; now we will tell its interpretation before the king. **(37)** You, O king, are the king of kings, to whom the God of heaven has given the kingdom, the power, the strength and the glory; **(38)** and wherever the sons of men dwell, *or* the beasts of the field, or the birds of the sky, He has given *them* into your hand and has caused you to rule over them all. You are the head of gold.

(39) "After you there will arise another kingdom inferior to you, then another third kingdom of bronze, which will rule over all the earth. **(40)** Then there will be a fourth kingdom as strong as iron; inasmuch as iron crushes and shatters all things, so, like iron that breaks in pieces, it will crush and break all these in pieces. **(41)** In that you saw the feet and toes, partly of potter's clay and partly of iron, it will be a divided kingdom; but it will have in it the toughness of iron, inasmuch as you saw the iron mixed with common clay. **(42)** *As* the toes of the feet *were* partly of iron and partly of pottery, *so* some of the kingdom will be strong and part of it will be brittle. **(43)** And in that you saw the iron mixed with common clay, they will combine with one another in the seed of men; but they will not adhere to one another, even as iron does not combine with pottery.

(44) "In the days of those kings the God of heaven will set up a kingdom which will never be destroyed, and *that* kingdom will not be left for another people; it will crush and put an end to all these kingdoms, but it will itself endure forever. **(45)** Inasmuch as you saw that a stone was cut out of the mountain without hands and that it crushed the iron, the bronze, the clay, the silver and the gold, the great God has made known to the king what will take place in the future; so the dream is true and its interpretation is trustworthy."

(46) Then King Nebuchadnezzar fell on his face and did homage to Daniel, and gave orders to present to him an offering and fragrant incense. **(47)** The king answered Daniel and said, "Surely your God is a God of gods and a Lord of kings and a revealer of mysteries, since you have been able to reveal this mystery." **(48)** Then the king promoted Daniel and gave him many great gifts, and he made him ruler over the whole province of Babylon and chief prefect over all the wise men of Babylon. **(49)** And Daniel made request of the king, and he appointed Shadrach, Meshach and Abed-nego over the administration of the province of Babylon, while Daniel was at the king's court.

How amazing that God revealed the future to Nebuchadnezzar! Using an enormous statue for the image, God showed Nebuchadnezzar a picture representation of how the succession of earthly kingdoms would occur. Babylon would be the greatest, and those which were to follow would progressively become more inferior. Much has been written concerning the intricacies of this dream's meaning, and scholars seem to believe the kingdoms represented are these:

- Head of the statue made of gold—Babylon
- Chest and arms made of silver—Medo-Persia
- Belly and thighs made of bronze—Greece
- Legs made of iron—Rome
- Feet and toes made of part clay and part iron—possibly the 10 provinces of Rome[1]

Up until this dream, it's likely Nebuchadnezzar knew nothing of God's plan for his life. Think how this mighty ruler felt upon learning his great successes were due to God's favor rather than his own efforts! With this dream, God made sure Nebuchadnezzar knew He had chosen him. As Daniel explained, it was God who had placed the king in this high position and given him such great power.

God reveals the coming of Christ and His divine kingdom.

But as amazing as it was that God revealed the coming earthly kingdoms, it was even more amazing that God should reveal His divine plan for His eternal kingdom. And He revealed it to Nebuchadnezzar, of all people. This pagan ruler, the one who had conquered the Israelites and led them off into captivity, was given a vision of Jesus and His eternal reign.

Like a video playing in Nebuchadnezzar's mind, the dream showed a stone being cut—without human hands—from the mountain. This stone would crush all the earthly kingdoms. It would grow into a mountain and fill the whole earth. This

---

— 1 —

Nebuchadnezzar's Dream. Search online for "kingdoms in Nebuchadnezzar's dream" and view "images" to see various depictions of the great statue and the kingdoms represented by the parts of the body. There does not seem to be a consensus on the feet mixed with iron and clay.

divinely created new kingdom would replace all the earthly kingdoms, and it would endure forever. That stone, of course, would be Jesus Christ, and with His death and resurrection, He would establish God's divine and eternal kingdom, once and for all time.

Nebuchadnezzar knew that Daniel spoke the truth. Greatly humbled by God's revelation to him, he fell to the floor and gave God the glory. What an impact this made on Nebuchadnezzar! Well, at least for the time being.

Can you imagine being selected by God to be part of His plan and being shown the future of the world? Well, actually, God has extended that same privilege and honor to Christians through the ages, and He still extends it today. To better understand, read Paul's explanation of God's beautiful plan in the first chapter of his letter to the Ephesians. Before He even created the world, God decided to adopt those who would be united with Christ into His own family. Yes, believers are part of God's eternal plan!

"For God so loved the world that he gave his one and only Son, that whoever believes in him shall not perish but have eternal life."
(John 3:16 NIV)

Thoughts to Ponder

Why do you suppose God revealed to Nebuchadnezzar the coming of Christ? How was his kingdom like the head of gold in the statue?

_____

_____

_____

_____

Read the Parable of the Wicked Tenants in Matthew 21:33–46. Note Jesus's reference to the stone the builders rejected and His explanation of the parable. How does this tie in with the happenings foretold in Nebuchadnezzar's dream?

_____

_____

_____

_____

In a relatively short period of time, Daniel went from his life hanging in the balance to being promoted ruler over the province of Babylon. What other examples can you think of where God turned a situation from being seemingly hopeless into an advantage for His people?

_____

_____

_____

_____

Chapter 10

King Nebuchadnezzar Forgets God

Scripture reference: Daniel 3:1–7 (HCSB)

(1) King Nebuchadnezzar made a gold statue, 90 feet high and nine feet wide. He set it up on the plain of Dura in the province of Babylon. (2) King Nebuchadnezzar sent word to assemble the satraps, prefects, governors, advisers, treasurers, judges, magistrates, and all the rulers of the provinces to attend the dedication of the statue King Nebuchadnezzar had set up. (3) So the satraps, prefects, governors, advisers, treasurers, judges, magistrates, and all the rulers of the provinces assembled for the dedication of the statue the king had set up. Then they stood before the statue Nebuchadnezzar had set up.

(4) A herald loudly proclaimed, "People of every nation and language, you are commanded: (5) When you hear the sound of the horn, flute, zither, lyre, harp, drum, and every kind of music, you are to fall down and worship the gold statue that King Nebuchadnezzar has set up. (6) But whoever does not fall down and worship will immediately be thrown into a furnace of blazing fire."

(7) Therefore, when all the people heard the sound of the horn, flute, zither, lyre, harp, and every kind of music, people of every nation and language fell down and worshiped the gold statue that King Nebuchadnezzar had set up.

It's unknown how much time passed between the end of Chapter 2 and the beginning of Chapter 3, but during that time Nebuchadnezzar had a *big* lapse in memory! Back when Daniel had interpreted his dream for him in Chapter 2, he was greatly humbled. He understood that it was God who had placed him in his position of power and made his kingdom the greatest on earth. When Daniel revealed God's message to him, Nebuchadnezzar fell to the floor and gave God the glory, declaring, "Truly, your God is God of gods and Lord of kings …" (Daniel 2:47 ESV).

By Chapter 3, Nebuchadnezzar had already forgotten God's supremacy and made an image or statue of gold. Worse, he decreed that *everyone* must worship this idol. With this idol, he sought to wield his power over the lives of everyone in the kingdom. Obviously, he was not content simply to control their physical, day-to-day lives. He sought to control their inner spiritual being as well. And, with an iron hand, he demanded they comply—or else be burned alive in a fiery furnace.

What did it take to build such a statue? The size alone shows that it wasn't erected on a whim; much planning went into its creation. This enormous image measured about 90 feet high (27 meters or 60 cubits) by 9 feet wide (2.7 meters or 6 cubits). It would tower over the Christ of the Ozarks statue located near Eureka Springs, Arkansas, and over the Great Sphinx of Giza in Egypt, both of which stand only about 65 feet high (or about 20 meters or 43 cubits).

With dimensions ten times taller than its width, this statue would have required the efforts of skillful engineers and many workers. Without the cranes and heavy equipment used today, it would have taken some amount of time to erect, possibly several years.

And then, think of the resources that Nebuchadnezzar put into this statue. It was made of gold, the most precious of metals. We aren't told if it was constructed as a solid chunk of gold or if it was hollow in the middle. Even if it was only gold plated on the outer surfaces, the size of this statue tells us a great amount of gold was used in its creation. Imagine how dazzling it must have shone there on the plain of Dura.

Upon the completion of this image, Nebuchadnezzar held an elaborate dedication ceremony and summoned everybody who was anybody to attend. Then he issued his proclamation that everyone, regardless of nationality or language, must fall down and worship this image whenever certain music was played. If they refused, they would immediately be burned alive.

When things are going well, it's easy to forget God.

Certainly, Nebuchadnezzar was not the first—nor the last—person to forget God. Time and again, throughout the Old Testament, God's people would pledge their lives to Him and give Him great honor and glory, only to forget a short while later and turn to false gods.

As you read of the Israelites wandering in the desert wilderness for forty years, their forgetfulness of God's goodness and favor toward them became a predictable pattern. The same thing happened during the time of the prophets: They warned the people, who then turned from their wicked ways only to later forget their love and devotion to God. Often God's people would return to serving images they had made themselves or the false gods they had adopted from other people.

It's easy to forget God in today's world as well. When difficulties and trials arise, you may instinctively turn to the Rock, much as David did in Psalm 61:1–2 (KJV): "Hear my cry, O God; attend unto my prayer. From the end of the earth will I cry unto thee, when my heart is overwhelmed: lead me to the rock that is higher than I." But when the situation eases, when the conflict is resolved, when the storm has passed—then what do you do? It's so easy to just go on about your way.

How can you keep God always in the forefront of your thoughts? One thing that can help is to make praise and thankfulness a daily habit. Singing songs to God or listening to Christian music not only turns your heart toward Him but also lifts your spirit. Keeping a thankfulness journal and every day recording several things for which you're thankful can be truly impactful. As you fill your journal, realize that you hold in your hand a tangible reminder of God's favor in your life. Know that God's love toward you never wavers. Daily seek to remember His goodness!

Give thanks to the Lord, for he is good; his love endures forever. Let the redeemed of the Lord tell their story …. Let them give thanks to the Lord for his unfailing love and his wonderful deeds for mankind ….

(Psalm 107:1–2, 8 NIV)

Thoughts to Ponder

What does the golden image that Nebuchadnezzar built and his commands concerning it reveal about his character?

_____

_____

_____

_____

What other powerful military conquerors through the ages come to mind? How were they similar or dissimilar to Nebuchadnezzar?

_____

_____

_____

_____

Do you think Daniel and his fellow Jews knew the intent of the king concerning this image during the time it was being built? How do you think they felt as its completion drew near?

_____

_____

_____

_____

Chapter 11

Risking Their Lives to Honor God

Scripture reference: Daniel 3:8–30 (NIV)

(8) At this time some astrologers came forward and denounced the Jews. **(9)** They said to King Nebuchadnezzar, "May the king live forever! **(10)** Your Majesty has issued a decree that everyone who hears the sound of the horn, flute, zither, lyre, harp, pipe and all kinds of music must fall down and worship the image of gold, **(11)** and that whoever does not fall down and worship will be thrown into a blazing furnace. **(12)** But there are some Jews whom you have set over the affairs of the province of Babylon—Shadrach, Meshach and Abednego—who pay no attention to you, Your Majesty. They neither serve your gods nor worship the image of gold you have set up."

(13) Furious with rage, Nebuchadnezzar summoned Shadrach, Meshach and Abednego. So these men were brought before the king, **(14)** and Nebuchadnezzar said to them, "Is it true, Shadrach, Meshach and Abednego, that you do not serve my gods or worship the image of gold I have set up? **(15)** Now when you hear the sound of the horn, flute, zither, lyre, harp, pipe and all kinds of music, if you are ready to fall down and worship the image I made, very good. But if you do not worship it, you will be thrown immediately into a blazing furnace. Then what god will be able to rescue you from my hand?"

(16) Shadrach, Meshach and Abednego replied to him, "King Nebuchadnezzar, we do not need to defend ourselves before you in this matter. **(17)** If we are thrown into the blazing furnace, the God we serve is able to deliver us from it, and he will deliver us from Your Majesty's hand. **(18)** But even if he does not, we want you to know, Your Majesty, that we will not serve your gods or worship the image of gold you have set up."

(19) Then Nebuchadnezzar was furious with Shadrach, Meshach and Abednego, and his attitude toward them changed. He ordered the furnace heated seven times hotter than usual **(20)** and commanded some of the strongest soldiers in his army to tie up Shadrach, Meshach and Abednego and throw them into the blazing furnace. **(21)** So these men, wearing their robes, trousers, turbans and other clothes, were bound and thrown into the blazing furnace. **(22)** The king's command was so urgent and the furnace so hot that the flames of the fire killed the soldiers who took up Shadrach, Meshach and Abednego, **(23)** and these three men, firmly tied, fell into the blazing furnace.

(24) Then King Nebuchadnezzar leaped to his feet in amazement and asked his advisers, "Weren't there three men that we tied up and threw into the fire?" They replied, "Certainly, Your Majesty." **(25)** He said, "Look! I see four men walking around in the fire, unbound and unharmed, and the fourth looks like a son of the gods." **(26)** Nebuchadnezzar then approached the opening of the blazing furnace and shouted, "Shadrach, Meshach and Abednego, servants of the Most High God, come out! Come here!" So Shadrach, Meshach and Abednego came out of the fire, **(27)** and the satraps, prefects, governors and royal advisers crowded around them. They saw that the fire had not harmed their bodies, nor was a hair of their heads singed; their robes were not scorched, and there was no smell of fire on them.

(28) Then Nebuchadnezzar said, "Praise be to the God of Shadrach, Meshach and Abednego, who has sent his angel and rescued his servants! They trusted in him and defied the king's command and were willing to give up their lives rather than serve or worship any god except their own God. **(29)** Therefore I decree that the people of any nation or language who say anything against the God of Shadrach, Meshach and Abednego be cut into pieces and their houses be turned into piles of rubble, for no other god can save in this way." **(30)** Then the king promoted Shadrach, Meshach and Abednego in the province of Babylon.

Have you ever had someone who, on purpose, tried to get you into trouble? That was precisely the intent of the astrologers who told King Nebuchadnezzar that Shadrach, Meshach, and Abednego were not following his decree and worshipping the image he had erected.

These Jewish men had come to Babylon as captives, yet the king had placed them in positions of great authority. Even worse, the king himself knew they possessed true wisdom from God, unlike the other astrologers and "wise men" in the kingdom. What a perfect opportunity the king's decree provided these astrologers to have Shadrach, Meshach, and Abednego permanently removed from the scene!

Always choose to do the right thing, no matter what.

When faced with what appeared to be certain death, Shadrach, Meshach, and Abednego held to their faith. They put their trust in God and in His great power. Their devotion to God was so great they went so far as to tell the king that even if God chose *not* to deliver them, they would still refuse to worship the king's image (Daniel 3:18).

Talk about fanning the flames! The faithfulness of these three to God so infuriated the king that he ordered the furnace to be made seven times hotter than usual. It was so hot that it killed the soldiers who threw them into the fire. Yet, Shadrach, Meshach, and Abednego escaped totally unharmed, without even the smell of smoke on their clothes.

Once again, Nebuchadnezzar witnessed the amazing power of God, and once again he praised Him. Going forward, he ordered anyone who would dare speak against God be killed and their homes destroyed. As for Shadrach, Meshach, and Abednego, they came out even better than before. The king recognized them for the great courage they showed in defying his command and promoted them to even higher positions.

Just as God cared for these three men long ago, He cares for His faithful today. Bad things may happen, and difficulties will surely occur in life, but, like Shadrach, Meshach, and Abednego, always choose to do the right thing. Remember that the children of God are never alone, even when they must walk through the fire.

Where can I go from your Spirit? Where can I flee from your presence? If I go up to the heavens, you are there; if I make my bed in the depths, you are there. If I rise on the wings of the dawn, if I settle on the far side of the sea, even there your hand will guide me, your right hand will hold me fast.
(Psalm 139:7–10 NIV)

Thoughts to Ponder

Reread verses 16–18 and consider what a powerful statement these men made in the face of certain death. Have you known someone who exhibited such resolve?

_____

_____

_____

_____

How would it affect you if you had to live from day to day under the rule of someone who created life-or-death situations for you and who was given to such rage?

_____

_____

_____

_____

Does God always deliver His people from death? Why or why not? Consider Stephen and other early Christians. (See Acts 7:54–8:3.)

_____

_____

_____

_____

Chapter 12

The King's Second Dream— God Tries Again

Scripture reference: Daniel 4:1–18 (HCSB)

(1) King Nebuchadnezzar,

To those of every people, nation, and language, who live in all the earth:

May your prosperity increase. (2) I am pleased to tell you about the miracles and wonders the Most High God has done for me.

(3)   How great are His miracles,
    and how mighty His wonders!

    His kingdom is an eternal kingdom,
    and His dominion is from generation to generation.

(4) I, Nebuchadnezzar, was at ease in my house and flourishing in my palace. (5) I had a dream, and it frightened me; while in my bed, the images and visions in my mind alarmed me. (6) So I issued a decree to bring all the wise men of Babylon to me in order that they might make the dream's interpretation known to me. (7) When the diviner-priests, mediums, Chaldeans, and astrologers came in, I told them the dream, but they could not make its interpretation known to me.

(8) Finally Daniel, named Belteshazzar after the name of my god—and the spirit of the holy gods is in him—came before me. I told him the dream:

(9) "Belteshazzar, head of the diviners, because I know that you have a spirit of the holy gods and that no mystery puzzles you, explain to me the visions of my dream that I saw, and its interpretation. (10) In the visions of my mind as I was lying in bed, I saw this:

> There was a tree in the middle of the earth,
> and its height was great.

(11) The tree grew large and strong;
its top reached to the sky,
and it was visible to the ends of the earth.

(12) Its leaves were beautiful, its fruit was abundant,
and on it was food for all.

> Wild animals found shelter under it,
> the birds of the air lived in its branches,
> and every creature was fed from it.

(13) "As I was lying in my bed, I also saw in the visions of my mind an observer, a holy one, coming down from heaven. (14) He called out loudly:

> Cut down the tree and chop off its branches;
> strip off its leaves and scatter its fruit.

> Let the animals flee from under it,
> and the birds from its branches.

(15) But leave the stump with its roots in the ground,
and with a band of iron and bronze around it,
in the tender grass of the field.

> Let him be drenched with dew from the sky
> and share the plants of the earth
> with the animals.

(16) Let his mind be changed from that of a man,
and let him be given the mind of an animal
for seven periods of time.

(17) This word is by decree of the observers;
the matter is a command from the holy ones.

> This is so the living will know
> that the Most High is ruler
> over the kingdom of men.
>
> He gives it to anyone He wants
> and sets the lowliest of men over it.

(18) "This is the dream that I, King Nebuchadnezzar, had. Now, Belteshazzar, tell me the interpretation, because none of the wise men of my kingdom can make the interpretation known to me. But you can, because you have the spirit of the holy gods."

Nebuchadnezzar had already encountered God's greatness on several occasions. He learned from his first divine dream that it was God who had made him a mighty ruler and given him such great power. For a time he honored God, but then he lapsed back into his prideful, self-serving ways. He commanded everyone worship the towering image of gold he had built or else be burned alive. When Daniel's friends walked out of the fiery furnace unharmed, the king once again witnessed God's amazing power and paid Him homage, at least for a while.

Now, while sitting at home in his palace, contented, prosperous and very self-satisfied, Nebuchadnezzar had another disturbing dream. Perhaps he had mellowed with age because, this time, he actually told his wise men the dream without issuing death threats. The king was confident Daniel would be able to interpret the dream for him.

God doesn't give up on us.

What a way to get Nebuchadnezzar's attention! With this dream, God revealed to the king that he would undergo a drastic transformation and become like an animal. God wanted him and everyone else to know that, without a doubt, God holds all power and control. It is He who gives the kingdoms on earth to whomever He chooses.

What did God want from Nebuchadnezzar? He wanted the heart of the king, and He wanted his lasting devotion, not his occasional devotion. He wanted Nebuchadnezzar to acknowledge that he was where he was and what he was because of God's great power, and not by his own might.

God doesn't give up on those living today, either. He repeatedly offers opportunities for individuals to come to Him. He seeks a lasting relationship with *you*, in particular, because He loves you so much. In fact, He sacrificed His son to save you. But the decision to come to Him, to become His adopted child, must be yours.

Do you perhaps allow your prideful self to get in the way of your lasting devotion to God? It's easy to become self-satisfied like Nebuchadnezzar did when things are going well. So stop and think—what has God done in your life? How can you honor God today? Consider His great love for you, say thank you, and *always* give God the glory.

See what great love the Father has lavished on us, that we should be called children of God! And that is what we are!

(1 John 3:1 NIV)

I will praise the name of God with song and magnify Him with thanksgiving.

(Psalm 69:30 NASB)

Thoughts to Ponder

What is the significance of the enormous tree in Nebuchadnezzar's dream? What does this tree reveal about Nebuchadnezzar and his kingdom?

_____

_____

_____

_____

What other trees have been mentioned in the Bible? Why were trees so important in ancient times?

_____

_____

_____

_____

In finding someone to interpret his dream, compare Nebuchadnezzar's actions concerning his first dream with this dream. Do you think the confidence Nebuchadnezzar now had in Daniel dampened the king's typically explosive nature?

_____

_____

_____

_____

Chapter 13

God Gives Nebuchadnezzar Time

Scripture reference: Daniel 4:19–37 (HCSB)

(19) Then Daniel, whose name is Belteshazzar, was stunned for a moment, and his thoughts alarmed him. The king said, "Belteshazzar, don't let the dream or its interpretation alarm you."

Belteshazzar answered, "My lord, may the dream apply to those who hate you, and its interpretation to your enemies! **(20)** The tree you saw, which grew large and strong, whose top reached to the sky and was visible to all the earth, **(21)** whose leaves were beautiful and its fruit abundant—and on it was food for all, under it the wild animals lived, and in its branches the birds of the air lived— **(22)** that tree is you, the king. For you have become great and strong: your greatness has grown and even reaches the sky, and your dominion extends to the ends of the earth.

(23) "The king saw an observer, a holy one, coming down from heaven and saying, 'Cut down the tree and destroy it, but leave the stump with its roots in the ground and with a band of iron and bronze around it, in the tender grass of the field. Let him be drenched with dew from the sky, and share food with the wild animals for seven periods of time.' **(24)** This is the interpretation, Your Majesty, and this is the sentence of the Most High that has been passed against my lord the king: **(25)** You will be driven away from people to live with the wild animals. You will feed on grass like cattle and be drenched with dew from the sky for seven periods of time, until you acknowledge that the Most High is ruler over the kingdom of men, and He gives it to anyone He wants. **(26)** As for the command to leave the tree's stump with its roots, your kingdom will be restored to you as soon as you acknowledge that Heaven rules. **(27)** Therefore, may my advice seem good to you my king. Separate yourself from your sins by doing what is right, and from your injustices by showing mercy to the needy. Perhaps there will be an extension of your prosperity."

(28) All this happened to King Nebuchadnezzar. **(29)** At the end of 12 months, as he was walking on the roof of the royal palace in Babylon, **(30)** the king exclaimed, "Is this not Babylon the Great that I have built by my vast power to be a royal residence and to display my majestic glory?"

(31) While the words were still in the king's mouth, a voice came from heaven: "King Nebuchadnezzar, to you it is declared that the kingdom has departed from you. **(32)** You will be driven away from people to live with the wild animals, and you will feed on grass like cattle for seven periods of time, until you acknowledge that the Most High is ruler over the kingdom of men, and He gives it to anyone He wants."

(33) At that moment the sentence against Nebuchadnezzar was executed. He was driven away from people. He ate grass like cattle, and his body was drenched with dew from the sky, until his hair grew like eagles' feathers and his nails like birds' claws.

(34) But at the end of those days, I, Nebuchadnezzar, looked up to heaven, and my sanity returned to me. Then I praised the Most High and honored and glorified Him who lives forever:

> For His dominion is an everlasting dominion,
> and His kingdom is from generation to generation.

(35) All the inhabitants of the earth are counted as nothing,
and He does what He wants with the army of heaven
and the inhabitants of the earth.

> There is no one who can hold back His hand
> or say to Him, "What have You done?"

(36) At that time my sanity returned to me, and my majesty and splendor returned to me for the glory of my kingdom. My advisers and my nobles sought me out, I was reestablished over my kingdom, and even more greatness came to me. (37) Now I, Nebuchadnezzar, praise, exalt, and glorify the King of heaven, because all His works are true and His ways are just. He is able to humble those who walk in pride.

◇◇◇◇

What if you were the one who had to explain this dream to Nebuchadnezzar? Here was a king prone to making death threats, who had attempted to burn Daniel's friends alive. It's no wonder Daniel paused as he took in the full meaning and then searched for the words to explain God's message to one of the most powerful rulers in the world.

Why did Daniel find this dream so alarming? What human has ever been treated like this, to take on the mind of an animal, eat grass like an ox, grow feathers like an eagle and claws like a bird? Daniel urged the king to turn from his sins by doing what is right and to show mercy to the needy. Perhaps with a change of heart and behavior, God would spare him from having to live like an animal for seven years.

The king must have heeded Daniel's advice, because God delayed the fulfillment of the dream. Eventually, however, Nebuchadnezzar's pride got in his way yet again. Twelve months later, while surveying his kingdom, he in essence said: Look what I have done! Rather than acknowledging the blessings God had bestowed upon him, he gave himself the credit.

God will hold your place for you.

Yes, Nebuchadnezzar was truly special. Even though God cut down this magnificent tree, he saved the stump and the roots. God held the king's place for him, and at the end of his sentence, restored him to his throne. His advisors and nobles again sought him out, and he became even greater than before. Finally, Nebuchadnezzar understood that, truly, it is God who is in control and able to humble the mighty and the proud.

God will hold your place for you today, just as He did for this great king so long ago. No matter your current position or lot in life, He has bestowed upon you special talents and blessings unique to you. But it's up to you to acknowledge Him, step into your place, and use your talents for His glory.

For it was You who created my inward parts; You knit me together in my mother's womb. I will praise You because I have been remarkably and wonderfully made. Your works are wonderful, and I know this very well.

(Psalm 139:13–14 HCSB)

And whatever you do, in word or deed, do everything in the name of the Lord Jesus, giving thanks to God the Father through him.

(Colossians 3:17 ESV)

Thoughts to Ponder

What has God done at other times to humble someone? Can you think of any other instance where God caused someone to live like an animal as he did Nebuchadnezzar?

_____

_____

_____

_____

Daniel advised Nebuchadnezzar to do what was right and be kind to the oppressed, which supposedly the king did during the year his punishment was delayed. Yet, what was the nature of his sin that caused God to follow through on his punishment?

_____

_____

_____

_____

Can you think of other examples where someone went through a great ordeal or suffering and, because of God's grace, ended up in as good or better position than when they started?

_____

_____

_____

_____

Chapter 14

King Belshazzar Sees the Writing on the Wall

Scripture reference: Daniel 5:1–12 (HCSB)

(1) King Belshazzar held a great feast for 1,000 of his nobles and drank wine in their presence. **(2)** Under the influence of the wine, Belshazzar gave orders to bring in the gold and silver vessels that his predecessor Nebuchadnezzar had taken from the temple in Jerusalem, so that the king and his nobles, wives, and concubines could drink from them. **(3)** So they brought in the gold vessels that had been taken from the temple, the house of God in Jerusalem, and the king and his nobles, wives, and concubines drank from them. **(4)** They drank the wine and praised their gods made of gold and silver, bronze, iron, wood, and stone.

(5) At that moment the fingers of a man's hand appeared and began writing on the plaster of the king's palace wall next to the lampstand. As the king watched the hand that was writing, **(6)** his face turned pale, and his thoughts so terrified him that his hip joints shook and his knees knocked together. **(7)** The king called out to bring in the mediums, Chaldeans, and astrologers. He said to these wise men of Babylon, "Whoever reads this inscription and gives me its interpretation will be clothed in purple, have a gold chain around his neck, and have the third highest position in the kingdom." **(8)** So all the king's wise men came in, but none could read the inscription or make its interpretation known to him. **(9)** Then King Belshazzar became even more terrified, his face turned pale, and his nobles were bewildered.

1

Belshazzar. For a commentary on Belshazzar and this historic event, see the 1906 text presented in the Jewish Encyclopedia.

bit.ly/2ITb4PR

---

(10) Because of the outcry of the king and his nobles, the queen came to the banquet hall. "May the king live forever," she said. "Don't let your thoughts terrify you or your face be pale. (11) There is a man in your kingdom who has the spirit of the holy gods in him. In the days of your predecessor he was found to have insight, intelligence, and wisdom like the wisdom of the gods. Your predecessor, King Nebuchadnezzar, appointed him chief of the diviners, mediums, Chaldeans, and astrologers. Your own predecessor, the king, (12) did this because Daniel, the one the king named Belteshazzar, was found to have an extraordinary spirit, knowledge and perception, and the ability to interpret dreams, explain riddles, and solve problems. Therefore, summon Daniel, and he will give the interpretation."

◇◇◇◇

God didn't bother with dreams for this king. It's the end of the line for the Babylonian kingdom, and the end of the seventy years of holding the Jewish people captive. God simply pronounced Belshazzar's death sentence, and did so in such a dramatic way as to become epic. When that hand appeared and wrote upon the wall, an expression for the ages was born.

Why did God deal so severely with Belshazzar? With Nebuchadnezzar, God had repeatedly offered the king opportunities to come to Him. Not so for Belshazzar, at least not that scripture mentions. Rabbinical literature suggests Belshazzar may have been even more treacherous than his predecessors. The Talmud and Midrash refer to this king's harsh oppression of the Jewish people.[1]

God also knows the hearts of people, and it appears He had seen no inclination on the part of this king to acknowledge Him. Certainly, Belshazzar purposely dishonored God when he ordered the gold and silver goblets from the temple in Jerusalem be brought in to his party. By using these items which had been dedicated to God's service to drink and pay tribute to their false gods, Belshazzar openly mocked the living God.

As an aside, Rabbinical literature (see reference above) suggests that Belshazzar threw this great banquet as a defiant celebration. He knew Jeremiah's prophecy that the Jewish exile would last seventy years, and he had calculated the years. Since the overthrow of Jerusalem, Nebuchadnezzar had reigned forty-five years, Evil-merodach for twenty-three years, and now Belshazzar for two years. This all added up to seventy, and since the Jewish people were still in Babylonian captivity, Belshazzar reasoned the prophecy must have been false. So perhaps this wasn't just any celebration. It could have been one of sacrilege, deliberately designed to taunt God.

God will not be mocked.

When Belshazzar saw what seemed to be a human hand appear and begin writing on the plaster of the wall, he knew he was doomed. Undeniably, such a miraculous event could only be performed by a higher power. The hand wrote up on the wall, close to the lampstand, so the words were likely visible to everyone there.

Can you envision the terror that struck this entire crowd of revelers? There they were, goblets in hand, brazenly drinking toasts to their gods, and a hand without a body appears out of thin air. It's safe to assume the color drained out of the face of everyone there, not just the king's. You can even hear the hush begin to work its way across the crowd. As certain people notice the hand, they nudge others nearby, whisper under their breath and point to the wall. Within moments, this party is over, and the only sounds are those of crickets and knees knocking. When the people find their voices once more, their cries are ones of distress and alarm.

The nature of God remains unchanged today. He is patient and long-suffering, and the depth of His love for mankind is unfathomable. Yet, there are things God will not tolerate, not in ancient times, and not today. He sees into the heart and knows the inclination of one's thoughts. When a heart becomes hard and holds no love for Him, He may choose to no longer extend His mercy. It's one thing to sin, but as this Babylonian king discovered, *God will not be mocked!*

It is a dreadful thing to fall into the hands of the living God.

(Hebrews 10:31 NIV)

But because of your hardness and unrepentant heart you are storing up wrath for yourself in the day of wrath, when God's righteous judgment is revealed. He will repay each one according to his works ….

(Romans 2:5–6 HCSB)

Thoughts to Ponder

How did God use this evil king for His purposes?

_____
_____
_____

Why do you suppose God used a human hand (or at least fingers) to write on the wall? Why not just have words appear, or perhaps speak in a loud voice from heaven? What was God's purpose in writing words that had to be interpreted?

_____
_____
_____

If you had been this king, what emotions and thoughts would have gone through your mind all on this one day, this day that turned out to be the last day of your life?

_____
_____
_____
_____

Chapter 15

The Night Prophecy Was Fulfilled

Scripture reference: Daniel 5:13–31 (HCSB)

(13) Then Daniel was brought before the king. The king said to him, "Are you Daniel, one of the Judean exiles that my predecessor the king brought from Judah? (14) I've heard that you have the spirit of the gods in you, and that you have insight, intelligence, and extraordinary wisdom. (15) Now the wise men and mediums were brought before me to read this inscription and make its interpretation known to me, but they could not give its interpretation. (16) However, I have heard about you that you can give interpretations and solve problems. Therefore, if you can read this inscription and give me its interpretation, you will be clothed in purple, have a gold chain around your neck, and have the third highest position in the kingdom."

(17) Then Daniel answered the king, "You may keep your gifts, and give your rewards to someone else; however, I will read the inscription for the king and make the interpretation known to him. (18) Your Majesty, the Most High God gave sovereignty, greatness, glory, and majesty to your predecessor Nebuchadnezzar. (19) Because of the greatness He gave him, all peoples, nations, and languages were terrified and fearful of him. He killed anyone he wanted and kept alive anyone he wanted; he exalted anyone he wanted and humbled anyone he wanted. (20) But when his heart was exalted and his spirit became arrogant, he was deposed from his royal throne and his glory was taken from him. (21) He was driven away from people, his mind was like an

animal's, he lived with the wild donkeys, he was fed grass like cattle, and his body was drenched with dew from the sky until he acknowledged that the Most High God is ruler over the kingdom of men and sets anyone He wants over it.

(22) "But you his successor, Belshazzar, have not humbled your heart, even though you knew all this. (23) Instead, you have exalted yourself against the Lord of heaven. The vessels from His house were brought to you, and as you and your nobles, wives, and concubines drank wine from them, you praised the gods made of silver and gold, bronze, iron, wood, and stone, which do not see or hear or understand. But you have not glorified the God who holds your life-breath in His hand and who controls the whole course of your life. (24) Therefore, He sent the hand, and this writing was inscribed.

(25) "This is the writing that was inscribed: MENE, MENE, TEKEL, PARSIN.

(26) This is the interpretation of the message: MENE means that God has numbered the days of your kingdom and brought it to an end.

(27) TEKEL means that you have been weighed in the balance and found deficient.

(28) PERES means that your kingdom has been divided and given to the Medes and Persians."

(29) Then Belshazzar gave an order, and they clothed Daniel in purple, placed a gold chain around his neck, and issued a proclamation concerning him that he should be the third ruler in the kingdom. (30) That very night Belshazzar the king of the Chaldeans was killed, (31) and Darius the Mede received the kingdom at the age of 62.

By now, Daniel is an old man. As the seventy years of Babylonian captivity for the Jewish people draw to a close, it's fitting that Daniel, who was there from the beginning should also be present at the end. Once again, he will serve as the mouthpiece of God, personally proclaiming the final hours of the Babylonian kingdom and Belshazzar's rule.

Why didn't God just go ahead and strike dead Belshazzar and the blasphemous revelers? It seems God wanted them all to understand, without a doubt, that the events which were about to occur were directed by Him, the Living God. He dramatically captured their attention as He miraculously spelled out His judgment upon Belshazzar. With the inscription placed in such a visible spot and with so many people witnessing the hand, God's power and sovereignty could not be denied.

Undoubtedly, every eye in the banquet hall turned toward Daniel as the king's men ushered him into the room. The crowd likely parted before him as he calmly stepped before the king. This wise, old Jewish sage had stood before the powerful conqueror, Nebuchadnezzar, delivering God's messages, and now he would stand before Belshazzar, the last king of the great Babylonian empire.

It's likely the fear that gripped the room could almost be felt in the air, a sense of impending doom. Unimpressed by the riches and power offered him by the desperate king, Daniel proceeded to relate God's message to Belshazzar. For this king, today would be his judgment day. He knew of God's power and sovereignty and how He had dealt with Nebuchadnezzar, yet Belshazzar had refused to humble himself. Rather, he had sought to deny God, to mock and blaspheme Him. With his heart already hardened toward God, this king would not be given another opportunity to acknowledge Him.

God keeps His promises.

For the Jewish people enduring Babylonian captivity, it had been a long seventy years. Just when it seemed the time had passed and the Babylonians were still in power, God fulfilled His promise. He ended the reign of Babylon in one day, with Darius the Mede taking over the kingdom.

God still keeps His promises today. During times when you may think all hope is lost and you have been forsaken, if you look, you can see that beautiful Hand of God in it all. Like Daniel, have unwavering confidence in God, the Living God, the all-powerful Creator of the universe. Remember, He came through on His promise of a Savior, and He will come through on all of His other promises as well.

Who shall separate us from the love of Christ? Shall trouble or hardship or persecution or famine or nakedness or danger or sword? … No, in all these things we are more than conquerors through him who loved us. For I am convinced that neither death nor life, neither angels nor demons, neither the present nor the future, nor any powers, neither height nor depth, nor anything else in all creation, will be able to separate us from the love of God that is in Christ Jesus our Lord.

(Romans 8:35–39 NIV)

Thoughts to Ponder

Review some of the scriptures in Jeremiah where it was foretold what would happen during Babylonian captivity. Begin reading around Jeremiah 21, or search on "Nebuchadnezzar" in the book of Jeremiah. Write down what you notice about how what was foretold lined up with what occurred in Daniel.

_____

_____

_____

_____

Compare Daniel's demeanor with that of the acute anxiety of everyone else in the room, particularly the king. What gave Daniel his confidence? Why was he not worried he would be killed for delivering this devastating message?

_____

_____

_____

_____

Why do you suppose God wrote "MENE" twice in His message to Belshazzar?

_____

_____

_____

_____

Chapter 16

King Darius Regrets His Decree

Scripture reference: Daniel 6:1–14 (HCSB)

(1) Darius decided to appoint 120 satraps over the kingdom, stationed throughout the realm, **(2)** and over them three administrators, including Daniel. These satraps would be accountable to them so that the king would not be defrauded. **(3)** Daniel distinguished himself above the administrators and satraps because he had an extraordinary spirit, so the king planned to set him over the whole realm. **(4)** The administrators and satraps, therefore, kept trying to find a charge against Daniel regarding the kingdom. But they could find no charge or corruption, for he was trustworthy, and no negligence or corruption was found in him. **(5)** Then these men said, "We will never find any charge against this Daniel unless we find something against him concerning the law of his God."

(6) So the administrators and satraps went together to the king and said to him, "May King Darius live forever. **(7)** All the administrators of the kingdom, the prefects, satraps, advisers, and governors have agreed that the king should establish an ordinance and enforce an edict that for 30 days, anyone who petitions any god or man except you, the king, will be thrown into the lions' den. **(8)** Therefore, Your Majesty, establish the edict and sign the document so that, as a law of the Medes and Persians, it is irrevocable and cannot be changed." **(9)** So King Darius signed the document.

(10) When Daniel learned that the document had been signed, he went into his house. The windows in its upper room opened toward Jerusalem, and three times a day he got down on his knees, prayed, and gave thanks to his God, just as he had done before. **(11)** Then these men went as a group and found Daniel petitioning and imploring his God. **(12)** So they approached the king and asked about his edict: "Didn't you sign an edict that for 30 days any man who petitions any god or man except you, the king, will be thrown into the lions' den?"

The king answered, "As a law of the Medes and Persians, the order stands and is irrevocable."

(13) Then they replied to the king, "Daniel, one of the Judean exiles, has ignored you, the king, and the edict you signed, for he prays three times a day." **(14)** As soon as the king heard this, he was very displeased; he set his mind on rescuing Daniel and made every effort until sundown to deliver him.

Think of how much wealth the king of Babylonia controlled. It's likely Darius the Mede, having taken over the kingship upon Belshazzar's death, didn't even know the extent of the riches and resources at his disposal. If the officials in charge discretely helped themselves to a little, the king would never miss it. Only Daniel stood in their way. Proficient, capable, and honest, he kept an accurate record of everything. He couldn't be bribed, and he couldn't be blackmailed. Worse, the king planned to place him in charge of the entire kingdom.

These administrators knew the only way they could ensnare Daniel would be through his devotion to God. By playing off King Darius's ego and pride, they set a trap for him. They proposed that for thirty days, people could pray only to the king. Darius, thinking only of the glory and adoration he would receive, failed to consider the consequences.

Always do the right thing, no matter what.

Undoubtedly, Daniel knew the motive of these administrators in getting such a decree approved. Having worked with them frequently, if not every day, he knew the makeup of their character. He knew this action was aimed directly at him, and he knew the penalty would be a gruesome death.

Still, Daniel's faith in his God never wavered. He prayed, just as he had before, fully aware he would be seen by those seeking to destroy him. Worshipping and honoring God mattered to him far more than the threat of capture. After all, he and his friends had personally witnessed God's power and His mighty deliverance. Depending fully on His faithfulness, Daniel decided that, whether he was to live or whether he was to die, his trust would be in God.

Think of the peace such faith can, and does, provide today. Make the decision, once and for all, to trust completely in Him, and you will *never* have to worry! Recall the powerful words of faith spoken by Shadrach, Meshach, and Abednego as they faced what should have been their certain death in the fiery furnace:

> King Nebuchadnezzar, we do not need to defend ourselves before you in this matter. If we are thrown into the blazing furnace, the God we serve is able to deliver us from it, and he will deliver us from Your Majesty's hand. **But even if he does not, we want you to know, Your Majesty, that we will not serve your gods or worship the image of gold you have set up.**
>
> (Daniel 3:16–18 NIV)

Believers through the ages have lived by these words, choosing to serve God rather than man. Sometimes they have been delivered from death, but other times they have not. Many have been forced to endure severe persecution and suffered agonizing deaths.[1] Yet death holds no power over the faithful, for God's people know eternal life is promised to all who put their faith in Him and His Son, Jesus. Thanks be to our loving Savior who conquered death once and for all time!

— 1 —

Nero Caesar and the Christian Faith. This article discusses the great persecution of the early Christians.

bit.ly/2kObuG4

Death has been swallowed up in victory. Death, where is your victory? Death, where is your sting?
(1 Corinthians 15:54b–55 HCSB)

"These things I have spoken to you, so that in Me you may have peace. In the world you have tribulation, but take courage; I have overcome the world."
(John 16:33 NASB)

The eyes of the Lord are upon the righteous, and his ears are open unto their cry. The face of the Lord is against them that do evil, to cut off the remembrance of them from the earth.
(Psalm 34:15–16 KJV)

Thoughts to Ponder

What does it say about King Darius that he would go along with a decree that people could pray only to him?

_____

_____

_____

_____

What does it say about the other officials that they would even suggest such a decree be made?

_____

_____

_____

_____

Why do you think the other officials wanted Daniel out of the way? Were they simply trying to advance their own political ambitions by tearing someone else down? Might they have been afraid of what Daniel would uncover about the way they had been handling government assets if he were placed in charge of the whole kingdom?

_____

_____

_____

_____

Chapter 17

God Saves Daniel from Death

Scripture reference: Daniel 6:13–28 (HCSB)

(13) Then they replied to the king, "Daniel, one of the Judean exiles, has ignored you, the king, and the edict you signed, for he prays three times a day." (14) As soon as the king heard this, he was very displeased; he set his mind on rescuing Daniel and made every effort until sundown to deliver him.

(15) Then these men went to the king and said to him, "You as king know it is a law of the Medes and Persians that no edict or ordinance the king establishes can be changed."

(16) So the king gave the order, and they brought Daniel and threw him into the lions' den. The king said to Daniel, "May your God, whom you serve continually, rescue you!" (17) A stone was brought and placed over the mouth of the den. The king sealed it with his own signet ring and with the signet rings of his nobles, so that nothing in regard to Daniel could be changed. (18) Then the king went to his palace and spent the night fasting. No diversions were brought to him, and he could not sleep.

(19) At the first light of dawn the king got up and hurried to the lions' den. (20) When he reached the den, he cried out in anguish to Daniel. "Daniel, servant of the living God," the king said, "has your God whom you serve continually been able to rescue you from the lions?"

(21) Then Daniel spoke with the king: "May the king live forever. (22) My God sent His angel and shut the lions' mouths. They haven't hurt me, for I was found innocent before Him. Also, I have not committed a crime against you my king."

(23) The king was overjoyed and gave orders to take Daniel out of the den. So Daniel was taken out of the den, uninjured, for he trusted in his God. (24) The king then gave the command, and those men who had maliciously accused Daniel were brought and thrown into the lions' den—they, their children, and their wives. They had not reached the bottom of the den before the lions overpowered them and crushed all their bones.

(25) Then King Darius wrote to those of every people, nation, and language who live in all the earth: "May your prosperity abound. (26) I issue a decree that in all my royal dominion, people must tremble in fear before the God of Daniel:

> For He is the living God,
> and He endures forever;
>
> His kingdom will never be destroyed,
> and His dominion has no end.

(27)   He rescues and delivers;

> He performs signs and wonders
> in the heavens and on the earth,
> for He has rescued Daniel
> from the power of the lions."

(28) So Daniel prospered during the reign of Darius and the reign of Cyrus the Persian.

Have you ever said or done something you regretted, and immediately you felt that sinking feeling in the pit of your stomach? The moment Daniel's name was spoken, King Darius must have realized he had made a mistake in issuing the decree for people to pray to him. And he instantly understood that he had been duped by the administrators whose jealous motive was to harm Daniel.

Darius tried in vain to think of ways to save Daniel. The laws of the Medes and Persians could not be altered, even by the king who issued them. His heart must have been heavy and filled with sorrow as he ordered Daniel thrown into the den of lions. Then he called upon God to protect Daniel, for he knew God would be Daniel's only hope.

Sleeplessness often follows regrettable decisions, and so it was with King Darius. By the first light of morning, he hurried to the lions' den to see about Daniel. Hoping against hope, he anxiously called out as he came near. Imagine the joy and relief he felt when he heard Daniel's voice answer in reply!

God's power and majesty are evident to all who will see.

Over and over, God had displayed His power to the Babylonian kings during the time the Jews were held in captivity. Now, He proved His might to yet another pagan king, Darius of the Medo-Persian Empire. Just as Nebuchadnezzar had done years earlier, Darius acknowledged and praised the living God.

Although many people today try to deny God's existence, His power and majesty can be felt and seen throughout all creation. From the vastness of the universe to the intricacies of the human body, the hand of God is evident in all. Look around you, observe His creation, and consider the many ways God is made evident in your life.

These beautiful words from Psalm 19:1–4a (NIV) are as true and relevant today as they were when penned many centuries ago:

> The heavens declare the glory of God; the skies proclaim the work of his hands. Day after day they pour forth speech; night after night they reveal knowledge. They have no speech, they use no words; no sound is heard from them. Yet their voice goes out into all the earth, their words to the ends of the world.

For His invisible attributes, that is, His eternal power and divine nature, have been clearly seen since the creation of the world, being understood through what He has made. As a result, people are without excuse.

(Romans 1:20 HCSB)

Thoughts to Ponder

If you were King Darius, what thoughts would race through your mind when you realized you had been trapped by your own decree?

_____

_____

_____

_____

If you were the other officials who had pulled this off, what would you be thinking and feeling when the king realized he had no choice but to follow through on his orders?

_____

_____

_____

_____

Do you think it ever occurred to these officials that the tables would be turned, and they would be the ones to suffer the gruesome fate they had planned for Daniel? Can you think of other instances where someone became ensnared by their own trap?

_____

_____

_____

_____

Chapter 18

Daniel Glimpses Eternity

Scripture reference: Daniel 7:1–14 (NLT)

(1) Earlier, during the first year of King Belshazzar's reign in Babylon, Daniel had a dream and saw visions as he lay in his bed. He wrote down the dream, and this is what he saw.

(2) In my vision that night, I, Daniel, saw a great storm churning the surface of a great sea, with strong winds blowing from every direction. (3) Then four huge beasts came up out of the water, each different from the others.

(4) The first beast was like a lion with eagles' wings. As I watched, its wings were pulled off, and it was left standing with its two hind feet on the ground, like a human being. And it was given a human mind.

(5) Then I saw a second beast, and it looked like a bear. It was rearing up on one side, and it had three ribs in its mouth between its teeth. And I heard a voice saying to it, "Get up! Devour the flesh of many people!"

(6) Then the third of these strange beasts appeared, and it looked like a leopard. It had four bird's wings on its back, and it had four heads. Great authority was given to this beast.

(7) Then in my vision that night, I saw a fourth beast—terrifying, dreadful, and very strong. It devoured and crushed its victims with huge iron teeth and trampled their remains beneath its feet. It was different from any of the other beasts, and it had ten horns.

(8) As I was looking at the horns, suddenly another small horn appeared among them. Three of the first horns were torn out by the roots to make room for it. This little horn had eyes like human eyes and a mouth that was boasting arrogantly.

(9) I watched as thrones were put in place
and the Ancient One sat down to judge.

His clothing was as white as snow,
his hair like purest wool.

He sat on a fiery throne
with wheels of blazing fire,

(10) and a river of fire was pouring out,
flowing from his presence.

Millions of angels ministered to him;
many millions stood to attend him.

Then the court began its session,
and the books were opened.

(11) I continued to watch because I could hear the little horn's boastful speech. I kept watching until the fourth beast was killed and its body was destroyed by fire. (12) The other three beasts had their authority taken from them, but they were allowed to live a while longer.

(13) As my vision continued that night, I saw someone like a son of man coming with the clouds of heaven. He approached the Ancient One and was led into his presence. (14) He was given authority, honor, and sovereignty over all the nations of the world, so that people of every race and nation and language would obey him. His rule is eternal—it will never end. His kingdom will never be destroyed.

You'll notice the content of the book of Daniel changes with Chapter 7. The first six chapters provide a record of historical events, and all the dreams documented there are those of other people. Beginning with this chapter, readers become privy to Daniel's own dreams, beginning with the Dream of the Four Beasts. And what a dream it is! With this video playing in his mind, Daniel is shown fantastically graphic displays depicting various struggles on earth and a judgment scene.

Who and what are the various beasts and kingdoms? The interpretations made through the centuries tend to vary with the reader's perspective. What's obvious from this terrifying account is that the struggle for power and control will both continue and intensify. How gratifying to know that no matter how great the struggles on earth, God is ultimately in control!

God is faithful to those who are faithful to Him.

No mortal prior to Daniel had ever been offered such an extensive view of what God had in store for mankind. Christians today recognize the references to God and to Jesus, who often referred to himself as the Son of Man. Like John, who centuries later recorded his visions in the book of Revelation, Daniel was given a glimpse into God's eternal realm.

Out of the many faithful who had lived earlier, why was Daniel allowed this special privilege? We can only speculate, but certainly his faith was part of the reason. Living almost his entire life in Babylonian captivity, he learned at an early age to depend totally on God. The prophet Ezekiel recognized Daniel, along with Noah and Job, for his righteousness in Ezekiel 14:14, 20 and spoke of his wisdom in Ezekiel 28:3.

Daniel also embodied the faith spoken of by the writer of Hebrews in 11:1 (NIV): "Now faith is confidence in what we hope for and assurance about what we do not see." Later in that chapter, the writer speaks of the great faith of the ancients: "By faith these people overthrew kingdoms, ruled with justice, and received what God had promised them. They shut the mouths of lions, quenched the flames of fire, and escaped death by the edge of the sword. Their weakness was turned to strength" (Hebrews 11:33–34a NLT). Without question, Daniel could be counted among this group of the faithful of old!

Christians today live by faith just as the ancients did. The lives of those who have gone before us serve as examples shining through the centuries. When you read the scriptures, you can see the faithfulness of God toward those who were faithful to Him. You can take heart, knowing the same God is still in control today. As you put your trust in Him, you can be confident that He will be faithful today and forevermore, just like He has always been.

Let us hold unswervingly to the hope we profess, for he who promised is faithful.
(Hebrews 10:23 NIV)

Thoughts to Ponder

How was the fourth beast different from the other beasts in Daniel's dream? How was its ultimate fate different?

_____

_____

_____

_____

How are the words spoken by the mouth on the horn of the fourth beast described? (Compare several versions of the Bible to get a better idea.) When does this mouth finally stop uttering these words? Do you sense relief when the words cease?

_____

_____

_____

_____

Describe the power represented by the beasts. Is their power peaceful? Is it lasting? Contrast their power with that of the Son of Man.

_____

_____

_____

_____

Chapter 19

Daniel's First Vision Interpreted

Scripture reference: Daniel 7:15–28 (NLT)

(15) I, Daniel, was troubled by all I had seen, and my visions terrified me. **(16)** So I approached one of those standing beside the throne and asked him what it all meant. He explained it to me like this: **(17)** "These four huge beasts represent four kingdoms that will arise from the earth. **(18)** But in the end, the holy people of the Most High will be given the kingdom, and they will rule forever and ever."

(19) Then I wanted to know the true meaning of the fourth beast, the one so different from the others and so terrifying. It had devoured and crushed its victims with iron teeth and bronze claws, trampling their remains beneath its feet. **(20)** I also asked about the ten horns on the fourth beast's head and the little horn that came up afterward and destroyed three of the other horns. This horn had seemed greater than the others, and it had human eyes and a mouth that was boasting arrogantly. **(21)** As I watched, this horn was waging war against God's holy people and was defeating them, **(22)** until the Ancient One—the Most High—came and judged in favor of his holy people. Then the time arrived for the holy people to take over the kingdom.

(23) Then he said to me, "This fourth beast is the fourth world power that will rule the earth. It will be different from all the others. It will devour the whole world, trampling and crushing everything in its path. **(24)** Its ten horns are ten kings who will rule that empire. Then another king will arise, different from the other ten, who will subdue three of them. (25) He will defy the Most High and oppress the holy people of the Most High. He will try to change their sacred festivals and laws, and they will be placed under his control for a time, times, and half a time.

(26) "But then the court will pass judgment, and all his power will be taken away and completely destroyed. (27) Then the sovereignty, power, and greatness of all the kingdoms under heaven will be given to the holy people of the Most High. His kingdom will last forever, and all rulers will serve and obey him."

(28) That was the end of the vision. I, Daniel, was terrified by my thoughts and my face was pale with fear, but I kept these things to myself.

As you read this account of Daniel's dream, do you wonder about the times we live in now? Are we currently living in one of these kingdoms to which this prophecy refers? Plenty of oppressive kingdoms and rulers have existed since the time this book was written, and students of the Bible have tried to match specific ones to those mentioned in this dream.

It's likely the true and complete meaning of this prophecy won't become clear until the end of time. Maybe God will explain it all to His faithful during eternity. On the other hand, maybe no one will care anymore. After entering God's glorious presence, earthly cares and struggles will be but a distant and fading memory!

This we do know, that evil is a very real and powerful presence on this earth, and that it will wage war against God's people until the bitter end. Although the faithful may be oppressed, trampled down, and forced to live under the rule of evil, this will last for only a period of time. And then it will be over.

Evil will be destroyed forever!

We live with the presence of evil every day of our lives. Bad things happen all around us and to us and to our loved ones. Within our hearts, we often struggle with hateful or impure thoughts. Evil is infused into our daily existence in myriad ways.

Can you imagine the amazing peace that will exist when there is no more evil? What will it feel like? Take a moment to envision it: no more death or destruction, no more hurtful words, divorces, or lawsuits. Your struggles without and within will be no more.

Absolute good will triumph. And it won't be up for discussion or debate. It will just BE—forever! All people and all rulers will universally recognize the sovereignty of our Lord Jesus to whom God the Father has given all authority on heaven and on earth. It will be as the apostle Paul wrote in Philippians 2:9–11 (ESV):

> Therefore God has highly exalted him and bestowed on him the name that is above every name, so that at the name of Jesus every knee should bow, in heaven and on earth and under the earth, and every tongue confess that Jesus Christ is Lord, to the glory of God the Father.

Beautiful words to commit to memory! Let them comfort you when you face struggles here on earth. You can know that absolute good—Absolute Love—will reign forever! Praise God for the gift of His Son. Praise God for His great love and mercy.

Praise God that the battle for our souls has already been fought and won by Jesus when He lived a life without sin. That upon His death, He descended into the depths of hell, paying the price for sin once and for all. That hell could not keep someone pure and without sin. That Jesus did not stay in the tomb, but arose on the third day. That He has gone to be with the Father and is preparing a place for His faithful!

When Jesus emerged victorious from the tomb, His everlasting kingdom began. All Christians can rejoice, because *they are already a part of that eternal kingdom!*

"All authority has been given to Me in heaven and on earth. Go, therefore, and make disciples of all nations, baptizing them in the name of the Father and of the Son and of the Holy Spirit, teaching them to observe everything I have commanded you. And remember, I am with you always, to the end of the age."
(Matthew 28:18b–20 HCSB)

Thoughts to Ponder

What do you suppose is the significance of the most terrifying beast being the fourth? What other groups of four are mentioned in the Bible?

_____

_____

_____

_____

How powerful is this fourth beast? Can the holy people defeat this beast on their own?

_____

_____

_____

_____

How do the holy people fare in the end?

_____

_____

_____

_____

Chapter 20

Daniel's Vision of the Ram and the Goat

Scripture reference: Daniel 8:1–14 (NLT)

(1) During the third year of King Belshazzar's reign, I, Daniel, saw another vision, following the one that had already appeared to me. (2) In this vision I was at the fortress of Susa, in the province of Elam, standing beside the Ulai River.

(3) As I looked up, I saw a ram with two long horns standing beside the river. One of the horns was longer than the other, even though it had grown later than the other one. (4) The ram butted everything out of his way to the west, to the north, and to the south, and no one could stand against him or help his victims. He did as he pleased and became very great.

(5) While I was watching, suddenly a male goat appeared from the west, crossing the land so swiftly that he didn't even touch the ground. This goat, which had one very large horn between its eyes, (6) headed toward the two-horned ram that I had seen standing beside the river, rushing at him in a rage. (7) The goat charged furiously at the ram and struck him, breaking off both his horns. Now the ram was helpless, and the goat knocked him down and trampled him. No one could rescue the ram from the goat's power.

(8) The goat became very powerful. But at the height of his power, his large horn was broken off. In the large horn's place grew four prominent horns pointing in the four directions of the earth. (9) Then from one of the prominent horns came a small horn whose power grew very great. It extended toward the south

---------- 1 ----------

Defining: Dispensation. Bible history can be divided into distinct periods of time, often referred to as "dispensations." The Patriarchal Dispensation existed from the time of the creation of Adam until the giving of the Law of Moses. During that era, God gave instruction to and dealt with the family heads of households, or patriarchs, such as Noah, Abraham, Isaac and Jacob. The Mosaical Dispensation began when God gave the children of Israel a written law. This Law consisted of the Ten Commandments as well as many other recorded laws (see the book of Leviticus). Then when Jesus came, He offered himself as the perfect sacrifice for sin, once and for all time. Thus, when He defeated death and rose from the grave, the Law of Moses was fulfilled. He ushered in the Christian Dispensation by establishing a spiritual, rather than an earthly, kingdom.

and the east and toward the glorious land of Israel. **(10)** Its power reached to the heavens, where it attacked the heavenly army, throwing some of the heavenly beings and some of the stars to the ground and trampling them. **(11)** It even challenged the Commander of heaven's army by canceling the daily sacrifices offered to him and by destroying his Temple. **(12)** The army of heaven was restrained from responding to this rebellion. So the daily sacrifice was halted, and truth was overthrown. The horn succeeded in everything it did.

(13) Then I heard two holy ones talking to each other. One of them asked, "How long will the events of this vision last? How long will the rebellion that causes desecration stop the daily sacrifices? How long will the Temple and heaven's army be trampled on?"

(14) The other replied, "It will take 2,300 evenings and mornings; then the Temple will be made right again."

Such a mysterious and complex vision! Perhaps, it should be called the Vision of the Horns. In this vision, God revealed to Daniel a greatly condensed version of the happenings that were to occur with earthly kingdoms in the years to come. This time period would be marked with devastating events for God's people: for them personally, for the way they worshipped, for all things sacred. (See verse 13.)

From our vantage point in time, this culmination seems to align with the fulfillment of the Old Law, or Mosaical Dispensation,[1] with Jesus establishing an eternal, heavenly kingdom. History records the catastrophic destruction of the temple and Jerusalem in AD 70. The early Christians endured a period of severe persecution, and any who survived fled to wherever they could find refuge. Indeed, great changes occurred during the years following Jesus's resurrection, and Christians began meeting together on the first day of the week rather than on the Sabbath, or seventh day.

Bible scholars vary in their interpretations of this vision. Even Daniel, the wise prophet of God, declared, "it was beyond understanding" (Daniel 8:27b NIV), and that was after the angel Gabriel explained it to him. Regardless, much can still be learned from studying this vision.

In this vision, God used symbols familiar to Daniel and the people of his day, namely animals and their horns. Horns represent the strength and power of an animal because they can use their horns as weapons, both to attack and to defend.

Sheep and goats were animals that provided sustenance for the people and were also offered as sacrifices. Sometimes, in scripture, they are referred to symbolically, with goats representing evil or those who are unsaved and sheep representing good or the saved. Jesus, who served as the perfect sacrifice for the sins of the world, is known as the Lamb of God.

Here in this vision, the goat is the evil aggressor. Not only does it trample the ram (or male sheep), which seems to represent an earthly ruler, but its power reaches to the heavenly realms as well. Truth is thrown to the ground, and the goat sets itself up to be as great as the commander of the army of the Lord. It takes away the elements of worship and tramples underfoot the Lord's people.

God's Word equips us to stand!

Great evil is present in the world today, and God's followers understand that it can last for only a period of time before good reigns victorious forever. But in the meantime, how are the faithful to withstand the waves of evil that keep coming, one upon the other?

Start by preparing yourself with studying the Bible, God's Word. Then make the decision to be faithful, regardless of your circumstances. Take courage in the knowledge that truth and goodness will overcome evil. And take to heart the following timeless instruction from the apostle Paul.

Worship in the Early Church. This article by S. Bracefield outlines the changes that occurred among the early churches as the worship practiced by Christians changed from Judaism to Christianity.

bit.ly/2kX70zu

Finally, be strong in the Lord and in his mighty power. Put on the full armor of God, so that you can take your stand against the devil's schemes. For our struggle is not against flesh and blood, but against the rulers, against the authorities, against the powers of this dark world and against the spiritual forces of evil in the heavenly realms. Therefore put on the full armor of God, so that when the day of evil comes, you may be able to stand your ground, and after you have done everything, to stand. Stand firm then, with the belt of truth buckled around your waist, with the breastplate of righteousness in place, and with your feet fitted with the readiness that comes from the gospel of peace. In addition to all this, take up the shield of faith, with which you can extinguish all the flaming arrows of the evil one. Take the helmet of salvation and the sword of the Spirit, which is the word of God.

(Ephesians 6:10–17 NIV)

Thoughts to Ponder

According to Jewish literature, Belshazzar reigned for two full years and was killed at the beginning of his third year, on that fateful night in which the hand appeared and wrote on the wall. His death also marked the end of the 70 years of Babylonian rule. Why do you suppose Daniel's vision occurred right around this important historical juncture in time?

_____

_____

_____

_____

Why do you think God chose to reveal the future to Daniel?

_____

_____

_____

_____

What was the impact of this revelation on Daniel? What about its impact on future generations?

_____

_____

_____

_____

Chapter 21

Daniel's Second Vision Explained

Scripture reference: Daniel 8:15–27 (NLT)

(15) As I, Daniel, was trying to understand the meaning of this vision, someone who looked like a man stood in front of me. **(16)** And I heard a human voice calling out from the Ulai River, "Gabriel, tell this man the meaning of his vision."

(17) As Gabriel approached the place where I was standing, I became so terrified that I fell with my face to the ground. "Son of man," he said, "you must understand that the events you have seen in your vision relate to the time of the end."

(18) While he was speaking, I fainted and lay there with my face to the ground. But Gabriel roused me with a touch and helped me to my feet.

(19) Then he said, "I am here to tell you what will happen later in the time of wrath. What you have seen pertains to the very end of time. **(20)** The two-horned ram represents the kings of Media and Persia. **(21)** The shaggy male goat represents the king of Greece, and the large horn between his eyes represents the first king of the Greek Empire. **(22)** The four prominent horns that replaced the one large horn show that the Greek Empire will break into four kingdoms, but none as great as the first.

(23) "At the end of their rule, when their sin is at its height, a fierce king, a master of intrigue, will rise to power. **(24)** He will become very strong, but not by his own power. He will cause a shocking amount of destruction and succeed

---

1

The Ram, the Goat, and the Horn. This article presents an interesting study on the vision recorded in Daniel 8.

bit.ly/2ITk0EI

Ancient Susa. These articles provide historical information concerning the ancient city of Susa.

bit.ly/2IQ02h9

bit.ly/2kXdXAp

---

in everything he does. He will destroy powerful leaders and devastate the holy people. (25) He will be a master of deception and will become arrogant; he will destroy many without warning. He will even take on the Prince of princes in battle, but he will be broken, though not by human power.

(26) "This vision about the 2,300 evenings and mornings is true. But none of these things will happen for a long time, so keep this vision a secret."

(27) Then I, Daniel, was overcome and lay sick for several days. Afterward, I got up and performed my duties for the king, but I was greatly troubled by the vision and could not understand it.

One of the oldest cities in the world provides the setting for this vision. Strategically situated along the Ulai canal, or river, Susa (see Daniel 8:2) stood as an important political center for numerous empires, including those of the Elamites, Persians, and Parthians. It was the city where Esther became queen of Persia, and it was there that Nehemiah served as cupbearer for Artaxerxes I. This ancient capital city, then, serves as a fitting site for the revelation to Daniel of the great political power struggles that were to come.[1]

The angel, Gabriel, provides the explanation of this vision. It's interesting to note that few angels are named in scripture, and in verse 16 of this reading, the Bible mentions Gabriel for the first time. His role seems to be that of serving as a messenger of God, and he is mentioned by name only two other times in the Bible. He appeared to Zacharias (Zechariah) in Luke 1:11–19 to tell him that he and his wife Elizabeth would have a son named John, and he appeared to Mary in Luke 1:26–29 telling her she would give birth to Jesus.

Gabriel told Zacharias in Luke 1:19 that he (Gabriel) stands in the presence of God. Can you imagine how you would feel if suddenly an angel, this heavenly being sent by God, came near to you? It terrified Daniel, who fell facedown on the ground. Of course, all of this was happening to Daniel within his vision.

Do you sometimes think you would like to know what's going to happen in the future? Would you even be able to function in the here and now, knowing what's around the bend? God's plan is so much greater than what humans can fathom. It's likely that trying to understand or see all that God knows would totally overwhelm the senses, much like Daniel's were when he saw this revelation. Consider these words from Isaiah 55:8–9 (NLT):

> "My thoughts are nothing like your thoughts," says the Lord. "And my ways are far beyond anything you could imagine. For just as the heavens are higher than the earth, so my ways are higher than your ways and my thoughts higher than your thoughts."

Trust in the Lord always and know that the future belongs to God!

Daniel glimpsed the future, and he was overcome. He lay sick and exhausted for several days, unable to function. And he only saw an abbreviated summary, something like a short movie trailer. A taste was all Daniel got, and even that was almost more than this man of great faith and character could withstand.

It's interesting to note Gabriel's instruction to Daniel after the vision ended: Keep it secret (or in other versions, seal it up). Throughout the centuries, volumes have been written attempting to identify all the players and interpret the intricacies of this vision. But even Daniel, with an explanation given him by an angel from God, wasn't expected to understand every facet of this fantastic vision or to dwell upon its meaning.

Even today, with so much information presented, it's easy to feel overwhelmed just reading Daniel's vision. Rather than speculate on the uncertainties, it helps to focus on the certainties: No matter how intense the struggle or how powerful the wicked become, ultimately evil will be destroyed. Holding onto this truth, God's people can live confidently, knowing that in the fullness of time, God and His great goodness will prevail!

Trust in the Lord with all your heart; do not depend on your own understanding. Seek his will in all you do, and he will show you which path to take. Don't be impressed with your own wisdom. Instead, fear the Lord and turn away from evil. Then you will have healing for your body and strength for your bones.

(Proverbs 3:5–8 NLT)

Thoughts to Ponder

In what ways do the visions of Daniel affirm how special he was to God?

_____
_____
_____
_____

Compare the portion of the previous vision in Daniel 7:23–27 with the portion of this vision in Daniel 8:23–25. What similarities do you notice?

_____
_____
_____
_____

After this vision, Daniel lay exhausted or sick for several days. Why do you suppose he was so worn out?

_____
_____
_____
_____

Chapter 22

Daniel's Prayer

Scripture reference: Daniel 9:1–19 (NIV)

(1) In the first year of Darius son of Xerxes (a Mede by descent), who was made ruler over the Babylonian kingdom— (2) in the first year of his reign, I, Daniel, understood from the Scriptures, according to the word of the Lord given to Jeremiah the prophet, that the desolation of Jerusalem would last seventy years. (3) So I turned to the Lord God and pleaded with him in prayer and petition, in fasting, and in sackcloth and ashes.

(4) I prayed to the Lord my God and confessed:

"Lord, the great and awesome God, who keeps his covenant of love with those who love him and keep his commandments, (5) we have sinned and done wrong. We have been wicked and have rebelled; we have turned away from your commands and laws. (6) We have not listened to your servants the prophets, who spoke in your name to our kings, our princes and our ancestors, and to all the people of the land.

(7) "Lord, you are righteous, but this day we are covered with shame—the people of Judah and the inhabitants of Jerusalem and all Israel, both near and far, in all the countries where you have scattered us because of our unfaithfulness to you. (8) We and our kings, our princes and our ancestors are covered with shame, Lord, because we have sinned against you. (9) The Lord our God is merciful and forgiving, even though we have rebelled against him; (10) we have not obeyed the Lord our God or kept the laws he gave us through his servants the

prophets. **(11)** All Israel has transgressed your law and turned away, refusing to obey you.

"Therefore the curses and sworn judgments written in the Law of Moses, the servant of God, have been poured out on us, because we have sinned against you. **(12)** You have fulfilled the words spoken against us and against our rulers by bringing on us great disaster. Under the whole heaven nothing has ever been done like what has been done to Jerusalem. **(13)** Just as it is written in the Law of Moses, all this disaster has come on us, yet we have not sought the favor of the Lord our God by turning from our sins and giving attention to your truth. **(14)** The Lord did not hesitate to bring the disaster on us, for the Lord our God is righteous in everything he does; yet we have not obeyed him.

(15) "Now, Lord our God, who brought your people out of Egypt with a mighty hand and who made for yourself a name that endures to this day, we have sinned, we have done wrong. **(16)** Lord, in keeping with all your righteous acts, turn away your anger and your wrath from Jerusalem, your city, your holy hill. Our sins and the iniquities of our ancestors have made Jerusalem and your people an object of scorn to all those around us.

(17) "Now, our God, hear the prayers and petitions of your servant. For your sake, Lord, look with favor on your desolate sanctuary. **(18)** Give ear, our God, and hear; open your eyes and see the desolation of the city that bears your Name. We do not make requests of you because we are righteous, but because of your great mercy. **(19)** Lord, listen! Lord, forgive! Lord, hear and act! For your sake, my God, do not delay, because your city and your people bear your Name."

Can you feel the intensity of Daniel's prayer? It's almost palpable! He knew from the prophet Jeremiah that Jerusalem was destined to lie in desolation for seventy years. Like a prisoner marking off the days of incarceration on the cell wall, Daniel had counted every year. Now elderly, he knew that what he had been waiting for almost his entire life should be at hand—the deliverance of his people and the restoration of Jerusalem.

Daniel was a prayerful man and regularly prayed three times a day. But his words in these verses were no ordinary prayer. In preparation for this special prayer, he fasted, depriving his body of nourishment, in order to totally focus on his petition to God. Deeply penitent, as if in mourning, he wore sackcloth and ashes.

Instead of immediately petitioning God as he began his prayer, Daniel first praised God. He recognized His power and acknowledged His faithfulness toward those who serve Him. Daniel understood he was approaching the throne of the Almighty, and he did so with great humbleness and respect.

In the body of his prayer, Daniel outlined the sins of the Jewish people. He included himself among the sinners, even though he had been a faithful servant of God, often under adverse conditions. He recognized that, collectively, God's chosen people, the people whom He had delivered time and again, had disobeyed by worshipping idols and ignoring His commands.

Daniel summed up his account of the sins of his people by acknowledging they justly received what God had promised. They knew God's commands from the Law of Moses and from the prophets, who had issued warnings repeatedly. Still, they chose to turn from God. Jerusalem, the holy city, lay desolate as a result of their disobedience and rebellion.

Great is God's mercy!

How profound is Daniels' statement in Daniel 9:18b (NIV), "We do not make requests of you because we are righteous, but because of your great mercy." With this, Daniel expresses his understanding of both the nature of man and of God. Indeed, the Jewish people were being disciplined, and quite severely, due to their *lack* of righteousness.

Daniel instead appeals to God's merciful nature. He pleads with earnestness for the forgiveness of his people and the cessation of God's wrath toward Jerusalem. This city had been chosen by God for His holy sanctuary, and it, along with the Jewish people, were bearers of His Name.

Today, Christians bear the name of God through Jesus Christ, the Lord and Savior of all mankind. The Spirit of God no longer dwells in earthly structures but within Christians themselves. God, in His great mercy, sent His Son, Jesus, who willingly paid the price for the sins of the world with His own blood. How great is God's love that He would go to such lengths to provide a way of salvation for mankind; how great is His mercy!

Our God is truly an awesome God, deserving of more gratitude than we will ever be able to express. May we, like Daniel, remember to approach Him in prayer with humility and respect, always giving thanks for the unfathomable love He has shown us.

I will praise You, O Lord, among the peoples,
And I will sing praises to You among the nations.
For Your mercy is great above the heavens, And
Your truth reaches to the clouds.

(Psalm 108:3–4 NKJV)

Thoughts to Ponder

Daniel witnessed firsthand the power shift which God had foretold earlier through His prophet, Jeremiah. The hand writing on the wall signaled the end of King Belshazzar and of Babylonian rule. Now, with Darius the Mede as king, Daniel knew it was time for those seventy years of punishment to be over. Why did Daniel feel compelled to pray this fervent prayer?

_____

_____

_____

_____

What insight does this prayer give you as to the depth of Daniel's character?

_____

_____

_____

_____

Was Daniel personally ever able to leave Babylon? (See Daniel 6:28.)

_____

_____

_____

_____

Chapter 23

The Seventy "Sevens"

Scripture reference: Daniel 9:20–27 (NIV)

(20) While I was speaking and praying, confessing my sin and the sin of my people Israel and making my request to the Lord my God for his holy hill— (21) while I was still in prayer, Gabriel, the man I had seen in the earlier vision, came to me in swift flight about the time of the evening sacrifice.

(22) He instructed me and said to me, "Daniel, I have now come to give you insight and understanding. (23) As soon as you began to pray, a word went out, which I have come to tell you, for you are highly esteemed. Therefore, consider the word and understand the vision:

(24) "Seventy 'sevens' are decreed for your people and your holy city to finish transgression, to put an end to sin, to atone for wickedness, to bring in everlasting righteousness, to seal up vision and prophecy and to anoint the Most Holy Place. (25) Know and understand this: From the time the word goes out to restore and rebuild Jerusalem until the Anointed One, the ruler, comes, there will be seven 'sevens,' and sixty-two 'sevens.' It will be rebuilt with streets and a trench, but in times of trouble. (26) After the sixty-two 'sevens,' the Anointed One will be put to death and will have nothing. The people of the ruler who will come will destroy the city and the sanctuary. The end will come like a flood: War will continue until the end, and desolations have been decreed. (27) He will confirm a covenant with many for one 'seven.' In the middle of the 'seven' he will

put an end to sacrifice and offering. And at the temple he will set up an abomination that causes desolation, until the end that is decreed is poured out on him."

Insight and understanding—that's what Gabriel said his explanation was supposed to provide. While he does offer a broad overview of future events, the specifics remain somewhat out of focus. Even from our vantage point today, several millennia farther down the timeline, many questions remain concerning the events he described.

In his special prayer, Daniel begged God to end the punishment of his people. Daniel had calculated the time which had passed, and he knew the seventy years of captivity God had decreed should be almost over. He fervently prayed for the Israelite people and for Jerusalem, the holy city God had chosen to bear His name.

God heard Daniel's prayer and immediately sent Gabriel to reassure him and to help him understand future events that were to unfold. While Daniel had prayed concerning the immediate future, God provided a much longer view that included the coming of the Anointed One or Messiah. God allowed Daniel to see how all the pieces of restoration and salvation were going to fit together.

This remarkable passage of scripture also illustrates the beautiful relationship that can exist between God and human beings. God cares deeply for us. We are His creation, His own handiwork. God longs for a personal relationship with each of us and makes Himself accessible to those who truly seek Him.

Even while the Jewish people were being punished with exile in Babylonia, God never forsook them. He sent them a special message through the prophet Jeremiah instructing them how to live and what to expect during this time. In Jeremiah 29:13 (ESV), God reassured the people that, even while they were in exile, He would be accessible to them: "You will seek me and find me, when you seek me with all your heart."

From his own life experiences, Daniel knew how much God cares for those whose hearts are turned toward Him. He saw how God had enabled him, a Jewish captive in Babylonia, to become one of the most powerful administrators in the land. When his friends should have died instantly from being thrown into the fiery furnace, God had delivered them unharmed. When his body should have been ripped to shreds by lions, God had shielded him.

Seek God with all your heart.

Daniel was someone who had devoted his life to seeking God. It's likely he had studied the scriptures and knew well God's promises to those who diligently seek Him, such as the one in Deuteronomy 4:31 (NLT): "For the Lord your God is a merciful God; he will not abandon you or destroy you or forget the solemn covenant he made with your ancestors."

So when Daniel made preparations for his special prayer and began earnestly petitioning God, God listened. He didn't even wait for Daniel to finish, but immediately sent His special messenger, the angel Gabriel, who had previously appeared to Daniel. What Gabriel stated in Daniel 9:23a (NIV) illustrates the beauty of Daniel's relationship with God: "As soon as you began to pray, a word went out, which I have come to tell you, for you are highly esteemed." Not only was Daniel devoted to God, but God was devoted to him!

How could there possibly be anything better than being esteemed by God? For some people, their relationship with God remains one-sided. They worship out of a sense of obligation or of fear. But those who truly seek God are able to experience a beautiful, reciprocating relationship. God *is* all powerful, but He is also a loving, devoted Father.

What would it take for *you* to be esteemed by God? The apostle Paul states in Acts 17 (see below) that He is not far from any one of us. In fact, Paul explains it's not random that you're living now. God appointed the time for you to live, your opportune time for seeking Him. That's how much He cares for you, the lengths to which He has gone to have a relationship with you. God longs for you and made the ultimate sacrifice of His son for you. If you truly seek Him, you, like Daniel, will find Him.

"From one man he made all the nations, that they should inhabit the whole earth; and he marked out their appointed times in history and the boundaries of their lands. God did this so that they would seek him and perhaps reach out for him and find him, though he is not far from any one of us."

(Acts 17:26–27 NIV)

Thoughts to Ponder

Daniel probably wanted the captivity of his people to be over immediately and Jerusalem restored. Yet, God took a longer view and sent Gabriel to explain His timeline to Daniel. Do you think Daniel understood what Gabriel was telling him?

_____

_____

_____

_____

Why do you suppose God chose to reveal this part of His plan to Daniel?

_____

_____

_____

_____

Think back over the great historical events and the turbulence through which Daniel had lived. God cared for him, supplied his needs and saw him through. In this reading, how does God comfort Daniel once again, even while revealing more turbulence ahead?

_____

_____

_____

_____

Chapter 24

Daniel's Vision of a Man

Scripture reference: Daniel 10:1–11:1 (NIV)

(1) In the third year of Cyrus king of Persia, a revelation was given to Daniel (who was called Belteshazzar). Its message was true and it concerned a great war. The understanding of the message came to him in a vision.

(2) At that time I, Daniel, mourned for three weeks. (3) I ate no choice food; no meat or wine touched my lips; and I used no lotions at all until the three weeks were over. (4) On the twenty-fourth day of the first month, as I was standing on the bank of the great river, the Tigris, (5) I looked up and there before me was a man dressed in linen, with a belt of fine gold from Uphaz around his waist. (6) His body was like topaz, his face like lightning, his eyes like flaming torches, his arms and legs like the gleam of burnished bronze, and his voice like the sound of a multitude.

(7) I, Daniel, was the only one who saw the vision; those who were with me did not see it, but such terror overwhelmed them that they fled and hid themselves. (8) So I was left alone, gazing at this great vision; I had no strength left, my face turned deathly pale and I was helpless. (9) Then I heard him speaking, and as I listened to him, I fell into a deep sleep, my face to the ground.

(10) A hand touched me and set me trembling on my hands and knees. (11) He said, "Daniel, you who are highly esteemed, consider carefully the words I am about to speak to you, and stand up, for I have now been sent to you." And when he said this to me, I stood up trembling.

(12) Then he continued, "Do not be afraid, Daniel. Since the first day that you set your mind to gain understanding and to humble yourself before your God, your words were heard, and I have come in response to them. (13) But the prince of the Persian kingdom resisted me twenty-one days. Then Michael, one of the chief princes, came to help me, because I was detained there with the king of Persia. (14) Now I have come to explain to you what will happen to your people in the future, for the vision concerns a time yet to come."

(15) While he was saying this to me, I bowed with my face toward the ground and was speechless. (16) Then one who looked like a man touched my lips, and I opened my mouth and began to speak. I said to the one standing before me, "I am overcome with anguish because of the vision, my lord, and I feel very weak. (17) How can I, your servant, talk with you, my lord? My strength is gone and I can hardly breathe."

(18) Again the one who looked like a man touched me and gave me strength. (19) "Do not be afraid, you who are highly esteemed," he said. "Peace! Be strong now; be strong. "When he spoke to me, I was strengthened and said, "Speak, my lord, since you have given me strength."

(20) So he said, "Do you know why I have come to you? Soon I will return to fight against the prince of Persia, and when I go, the prince of Greece will come; (21) but first I will tell you what is written in the Book of Truth. (No one supports me against them except Michael, your prince. (1) And in the first year of Darius the Mede, I took my stand to support and protect him.)"

The last three chapters of Daniel all pertain to this same vision. Chapter 10 provides the setting for the vision, Chapter 11 provides the prophecy concerning future events, and Chapter 12 provides the summation and final instructions to Daniel. This is Daniel's last recorded vision, and it offers a more in-depth description of events set to unfold in the immediate future.

Daniel marks the time of the vision by the year of the king's reign. In all, the happenings recorded in the book of Daniel span a time of about seventy years. He was carried into captivity as a young person, so by the time this vision occurred, he had to have been elderly. Daniel had spent a lifetime depending on his God, and the events recorded in this chapter further reveal the depth of their beautiful relationship.

In this vision, Daniel once again found himself in the presence of a divine being. Whether this "man dressed in linen" was an angel or Christ himself is not clear. What is clear is that Daniel was overwhelmed by the presence of this messenger from God. It was too much for his human senses to handle.

Yet again, Daniel is told in Daniel 10:11 he is highly esteemed. (Other versions say *greatly loved, treasured by God,* and *very precious to God.*) How could a mortal attain such an honor? The answer follows in verse 12—Daniel set his mind to gain understanding and he humbled himself before God. From the first day that Daniel did this, God heard his words and responded. God helped Daniel understand what was happening and why.

God can make us stand.

With the focus of this vision being on future events, it's easy to overlook the interaction between Daniel and God's messenger. The awesomeness of experiencing this vision, coupled with the presence of a divine being, completely overwhelmed Daniel. Sapped of his physical and mental strength, he felt weak and had difficulty speaking and breathing. What enabled Daniel to function during such great stress? This messenger from God touched him and helped lift him, and he was able to stand and to speak.

You can be assured that God helps His people today to stand, just as he helped Daniel and all those through the ages who have put their trust in Him. Don't wait for difficult circumstances to occur. Reach out to God daily. Draw upon His great strength and listen to His words of instruction and comfort as you read your Bible.

God desires a relationship with you. After all, you were so special that He sent His only Son as a sacrifice for you. He will enable you to stand—if you allow Him.

"Do not fear, for I am with you; Do not anxiously look about you, for I am your God. I will strengthen you, surely I will help you, Surely I will uphold you with My righteous right hand."

(Isaiah 41:10 NASB)

Thoughts to Ponder

Why was Daniel highly esteemed? Why did his words elicit such a response? (See Daniel 10:10–12.)

_____

_____

_____

_____

Why do you think Daniel mourned so deeply and so long after this revelation concerning a great war?

_____

_____

_____

_____

The one speaking to Daniel mentions several "princes" who evidently are engaged in various struggles. Does there seem to be a spiritual battle going on behind the scenes which humans are not able to see?

_____

_____

_____

_____

Chapter 25

The Future Revealed to Daniel

Scripture reference: Daniel 11:2–27 (NLT)

(2) "Now then, I will reveal the truth to you. Three more Persian kings will reign, to be succeeded by a fourth, far richer than the others. He will use his wealth to stir up everyone to fight against the kingdom of Greece.

(3) "Then a mighty king will rise to power who will rule with great authority and accomplish everything he sets out to do. (4) But at the height of his power, his kingdom will be broken apart and divided into four parts. It will not be ruled by the king's descendants, nor will the kingdom hold the authority it once had. For his empire will be uprooted and given to others.

(5) "The king of the south will increase in power, but one of his own officials will become more powerful than he and will rule his kingdom with great strength.

(6) "Some years later an alliance will be formed between the king of the north and the king of the south. The daughter of the king of the south will be given in marriage to the king of the north to secure the alliance, but she will lose her influence over him, and so will her father. She will be abandoned along with her supporters. (7) But when one of her relatives becomes king of the south, he will raise an army and enter the fortress of the king of the north and defeat him. (8) When he returns to Egypt, he will carry back their idols with him, along with priceless articles of gold and silver. For some years afterward he will leave the king of the north alone.

(9) "Later the king of the north will invade the realm of the king of the south but will soon return to his own land. (10) However, the sons of the king of the north will assemble a mighty army that will advance like a flood and carry the battle as far as the enemy's fortress.

(11) "Then, in a rage, the king of the south will rally against the vast forces assembled by the king of the north and will defeat them. (12) After the enemy army is swept away, the king of the south will be filled with pride and will execute many thousands of his enemies. But his success will be short lived.

(13) "A few years later the king of the north will return with a fully equipped army far greater than before. (14) At that time there will be a general uprising against the king of the south. Violent men among your own people will join them in fulfillment of this vision, but they will not succeed. (15) Then the king of the north will come and lay siege to a fortified city and capture it. The best troops of the south will not be able to stand in the face of the onslaught.

(16) "The king of the north will march onward unopposed; none will be able to stop him. He will pause in the glorious land of Israel, intent on destroying it. (17) He will make plans to come with the might of his entire kingdom and will form an alliance with the king of the south. He will give him a daughter in marriage in order to overthrow the kingdom from within, but his plan will fail.

(18) "After this, he will turn his attention to the coastland and conquer many cities. But a commander from another land will put an end to his insolence and cause him to retreat in shame. (19) He will take refuge in his own fortresses but will stumble and fall and be seen no more.

(20) "His successor will send out a tax collector to maintain the royal splendor. But after a very brief reign, he will die, though not from anger or in battle.

(21) "The next to come to power will be a despicable man who is not in line for royal succession. He will slip in when least expected and take over the kingdom by flattery and intrigue. (22) Before him great

armies will be swept away, including a covenant prince. **(23)** With deceitful promises, he will make various alliances. He will become strong despite having only a handful of followers. **(24)** Without warning he will enter the richest areas of the land. Then he will distribute among his followers the plunder and wealth of the rich—something his predecessors had never done. He will plot the overthrow of strongholds, but this will last for only a short while.

(25) "Then he will stir up his courage and raise a great army against the king of the south. The king of the south will go to battle with a mighty army, but to no avail, for there will be plots against him. **(26)** His own household will cause his downfall. His army will be swept away, and many will be killed. **(27)** Seeking nothing but each other's harm, these kings will plot against each other at the conference table, attempting to deceive each other. But it will make no difference, for the end will come at the appointed time."

Why did God reveal so much amazing information to Daniel? The coming of the Messiah had been foretold and awaited by the Jewish people for centuries. But, with many of God's chosen people now living in Babylonian captivity, Jerusalem desolated, and the temple desecrated, you can imagine they may have grown discouraged. The visions shown to Daniel helped the people understand God's plan. He was still with them during this trying and pivotal time in their history—and He had an even bigger plan for the future.

God is in control.

The great struggle for power, whether in the spiritual realms or on earth, seems to be an overriding theme in Daniel's visions. The battles and political events Daniel foresaw in this vision differ very little from what occurs today. The players may change, but not the elements—the battles, betrayals, alliances, tax collectors, intrigue, deceit, etc.

Through the ages, God has used earthly rulers and their positions of power to bring about His will. He allowed the Babylonians to carry the Jewish people into captivity as punishment. He hardened Pharaoh's heart so that He could show His power in delivering His people from Egyptian slavery (Exodus 9:16).

In all those trying times, God remained firmly in control. Today, you can rest assured, even when bad things happen and you don't understand why they are happening, God is still in control. He always has been through the ages, and He always will be.

Commit to the Lord whatever you do, and he will establish your plans. The Lord works out everything to its proper end—even the wicked for a day of disaster.

(Proverbs 16:3–4 NIV)

Thoughts to Ponder

How do you think you would feel if presented with so much information concerning the future? Is it any wonder Daniel needed help to speak and function?

_____

_____

_____

_____

What recurring theme(s) do you notice in this revelation?

_____

_____

_____

_____

Pick verses from this chapter's reading that you find particularly interesting or intriguing and research them in a Bible commentary. You can find numerous commentaries at www.biblestudytools.com/commentaries. (This would be a good site to bookmark for future reference.) Scroll down to the Matthew Henry Commentary, which has served as a classic through the centuries.

What did you learn of interest about the verses you picked?

_____

_____

_____

_____

Chapter 26

Difficult Times for God's People

Scripture reference: Daniel 11:28–45 (NLT)

(28) "The king of the north will then return home with great riches. On the way he will set himself against the people of the holy covenant, doing much damage before continuing his journey.

(29) "Then at the appointed time he will once again invade the south, but this time the result will be different. **(30)** For warships from western coastlands will scare him off, and he will withdraw and return home. But he will vent his anger against the people of the holy covenant and reward those who forsake the covenant.

(31) "His army will take over the Temple fortress, pollute the sanctuary, put a stop to the daily sacrifices, and set up the sacrilegious object that causes desecration. **(32)** He will flatter and win over those who have violated the covenant. But the people who know their God will be strong and will resist him.

(33) "Wise leaders will give instruction to many, but these teachers will die by fire and sword, or they will be jailed and robbed. **(34)** During these persecutions, little help will arrive, and many who join them will not be sincere. **(35)** And some of the wise will fall victim to persecution. In this way, they will be refined and cleansed and made pure until the time of the end, for the appointed time is still to come.

(36) "The king will do as he pleases, exalting himself and claiming to be greater than every god, even blaspheming the God of gods. He will succeed, but only until the time of wrath is completed. For what has been determined will surely take place. **(37)** He will have no respect for the gods of his ancestors, or for the god loved by women, or for any other god, for he will boast that he is greater than them all. **(38)** Instead of these, he will worship the god of fortresses—a god his ancestors never knew—and lavish on him gold, silver, precious stones, and expensive gifts. **(39)** Claiming this foreign god's help, he will attack the strongest fortresses. He will honor those who submit to him, appointing them to positions of authority and dividing the land among them as their reward.

(40) "Then at the time of the end, the king of the south will attack the king of the north. The king of the north will storm out with chariots, charioteers, and a vast navy. He will invade various lands and sweep through them like a flood. **(41)** He will enter the glorious land of Israel, and many nations will fall, but Moab, Edom, and the best part of Ammon will escape. **(42)** He will conquer many countries, and even Egypt will not escape. **(43)** He will gain control over the gold, silver, and treasures of Egypt, and the Libyans and Ethiopians will be his servants.

(44) "But then news from the east and the north will alarm him, and he will set out in great anger to destroy and obliterate many. **(45)** He will stop between the glorious holy mountain and the sea and will pitch his royal tents. But while he is there, his time will suddenly run out, and no one will help him."

What a prophecy this presents! Consider the character of the King of the North—a completely ego-driven conqueror, or so it would seem. "The king will do as he pleases, exalting himself and claiming to be greater than every god, even blaspheming the God of gods" (Daniel 11:36 NLT). With his heart set against the people of the holy covenant (verse 28), you can see that this conqueror is essentially waging war against God and God's people. When he loses heart and turns back, he vents his fury against the holy covenant, rewarding or showing favor to those who forsake it (verse 30).

Rather than simply destroying the temple, "His forces will rise up and desecrate the temple fortress. They will abolish the daily sacrifice and set up the abomination of desolation" (Daniel 11:31 HCSB). From historical accounts, swine and other unclean animals were offered as sacrifices on the altar in Jerusalem by Antiochus IV Epiphanes in 168 BC.[1] Yet, with all his power and riches, this king's time will come to an end like all the rest, and no one will help him (verse 45).

God has a plan.

If, as Paul states in Romans 13:1, the governing authorities are established by God, did God cause this King of the North to perpetrate such evil? No, because from the beginning, God created mankind with a free will. Adam and Eve chose to eat of the Tree of Knowledge even though God had instructed them otherwise. James explains in 1:13–15 that God tempts no one to do evil. Each person chooses his or her thoughts and actions; otherwise God would simply have created pre-programmed robots.

God did, however, use this King of the North, whose heart was already bent on destruction and self-exaltation, just as He had used Pharaoh centuries earlier (Exodus 9:16). Looking back, we can see how the destruction wielded by this evil king ultimately carried out God's intent.

From the beginning, God planned a way of salvation for mankind, but it was a plan that He enacted over a long period of time. At first, He developed relationships with individuals, such as Noah and Abraham. Then He expanded upon these relationships to include His chosen people, the children of Israel. Ultimately, His desire was to provide a way of salvation for all mankind and establish a relationship with each of His faithful.

---- 1 ----

1 Maccabees 1. Maccabees (in the DRA version of the Bible most commonly used by the Catholic church) further describes this king's evil and destruction.

bit.ly/2lc3cso

The War of the Jews. Josephus gives an account of Antiochus Epiphanes's atrocities (see Book 1, Chapter 1, Paragraph 2).

bit.ly/2kXdlW3

The Messiah would be that Way. With Jesus's coming, God fulfilled His plan and established His heavenly kingdom. Jesus, who is the Messiah, offered Himself as the perfect sacrifice for sin, once and for all. This meant that daily sacrifices would no longer be needed. Nor would the system of earthly priests be needed; Jesus serves as our high priest forever (Hebrews 7:11–28). The dwelling place of God's Holy Spirit would also change. It would now be within the hearts of believers rather than in earthly temples or structures made by man (1 Corinthians 3:16).

Consider the great changes that had to occur in the thinking and manner of worship for God's faithful who lived during the time of transition from the Old Law to the New. These changes ran counter to centuries of law and tradition. The evil king helped force these changes to occur by destroying the temple and abolishing the daily sacrifices. This major disruption in how God's faithful worshipped actually set the stage for ushering in the Christian era.

God desires a personal relationship with you. He planned a Way to make that possible. Jesus is that Way. Who would have thought God could use an evil king to help enact His beautiful plan? He used him to help prepare a path for the Way—*His Way for you!*

Jesus told him, "I am the way, the truth, and the life. No one can come to the Father except through me."

(John 14:6 NLT)

Thoughts to Ponder

In this vision, the king of the North was depicted as ruthless, ruling with brute force and driven by his own ambitions and immense ego. Why do you think he resorted to using flattery to influence God's people? (See Daniel 11:31–35.)

_____
_____
_____
_____

Referring to the passage above, who are the ones who will be able to resist the force and influence of this king? Will it be an easy time for these people? What will be their ultimate outcome?

_____
_____
_____
_____

After all the battles and the great struggle for riches and control, what will be the outcome of these earthly rulers? (See Daniel 11:40–45.) Do you sense the futility of these struggles? How might Matthew 16:26 apply to them?

_____
_____
_____
_____

Chapter 27

The End Times— Great Changes to Come

Scripture reference: Daniel 12:1–13 (NIV)

(1) "At that time Michael, the great prince who protects your people, will arise. There will be a time of distress such as has not happened from the beginning of nations until then. But at that time your people—everyone whose name is found written in the book—will be delivered. (2) Multitudes who sleep in the dust of the earth will awake: some to everlasting life, others to shame and everlasting contempt. (3) Those who are wise will shine like the brightness of the heavens, and those who lead many to righteousness, like the stars for ever and ever. (4) But you, Daniel, roll up and seal the words of the scroll until the time of the end. Many will go here and there to increase knowledge."

(5) Then I, Daniel, looked, and there before me stood two others, one on this bank of the river and one on the opposite bank. (6) One of them said to the man clothed in linen, who was above the waters of the river, "How long will it be before these astonishing things are fulfilled?"

(7) The man clothed in linen, who was above the waters of the river, lifted his right hand and his left hand toward heaven, and I heard him swear by him who lives forever, saying, "It will be for a time, times and half a time. When the power of the holy people has been finally broken, all these things will be completed."

(8) I heard, but I did not understand. So I asked, "My lord, what will the outcome of all this be?" (9) He replied, "Go your way, Daniel, because the words

are rolled up and sealed until the time of the end. **(10)** Many will be purified, made spotless and refined, but the wicked will continue to be wicked. None of the wicked will understand, but those who are wise will understand. **(11)** From the time that the daily sacrifice is abolished and the abomination that causes desolation is set up, there will be 1,290 days. **(12)** Blessed is the one who waits for and reaches the end of the 1,335 days. **(13)** As for you, go your way till the end. You will rest, and then at the end of the days you will rise to receive your allotted inheritance."

Imagine the anxiety of God's people who lived during Daniel's time. Living in Babylonian captivity, they longed for the day they could return to their own land and rebuild God's temple and the holy city of Jerusalem. Prophets had foretold the coming of a Messiah. With great anticipation, they awaited this promised leader, deliverer, Savior!

Yes, God's people longed for deliverance from their oppression, and they knew great changes were coming. Exactly how all this change would come about was still largely a mystery. Daniel, being esteemed by God, was given insight with this vision concerning what this great transition period would be like for God's people.

Fantastic events would occur. Multitudes who "sleep in the dust" (who had already died) would awaken (verse 2). Matthew 27:51–53 (NLT) records this happening at Jesus's crucifixion when He gave up His spirit:

> At that moment the curtain in the sanctuary of the Temple was torn in two, from top to bottom. The earth shook, rocks split apart, and tombs opened. The bodies of many godly men and women who had died were raised from the dead. They left the cemetery after Jesus' resurrection, went into the holy city of Jerusalem, and appeared to many people.

As an aside, the apostle Paul describes in 1 Thessalonians 4:16–17 (NLT) a similar glorious resurrection of God's people that will occur at the end of time as well:

> For the Lord himself will come down from heaven with a commanding shout, with the voice of the archangel, and with the trumpet call of God. First, the believers who have died will rise from their graves. Then, together with them, we who are still alive and remain on the earth will be caught up in the clouds to meet the Lord in the air. Then we will be with the Lord forever.

Dreadful events would also occur during this transition time: "There will be a time of distress such as has not happened from the beginning of nations until then" (Daniel 12:1 NIV). God's people would suffer greatly while being subjected to the rule of foreign leaders and nations. History records the great persecution of Christians that occurred after the coming of Christ and of Jerusalem being destroyed by the Romans in AD 70.[1]

God will see you through.

It's difficult to imagine what life was like for God's people during Old Testament times. They lived under a rigid, complex set of laws that demanded harsh punishments for certain sins. Sacrifices had to be made time after time, and a system of earthly priests was needed to serve as the intermediary between God and man. The Spirit of God resided in structures made by man—first the tabernacle, and then later, the temple in Jerusalem.

At Jesus's death, everything changed. His defeat of death and His resurrection from the grave means that Christians today live by *grace!* It was no accident that the curtain of the temple was torn in two, with the rip traveling from the top down to the bottom—from God down to man. No longer would there be anything to separate believers from God's presence.

1

The Romans Destroy the Temple at Jerusalem, 70 AD. This article references Josephus's account of the Roman assault on the temple.

bit.ly/1P7eyG5

The Jewish War and the Destruction of Jerusalem, AD 70. Scroll down past the sources to read more about this historical time. Other chapters in this book, *The History of the Christian Church, Vol. 1*, also provide a wealth of information.

bit.ly/2IXPngn

Yes, the change from the Old Law to the New would be monumental for God's people who lived during that time. Daniel's vision served as a reassurance that, although great turbulence was to come, God had a plan and would see His people through.

Living today, on the other side of this great transition, you can look back and see how things transpired according to God's plan. You also know that many trials and tribulations are still to come. Rest assured, however, that whatever dreadful and fantastic events may lie ahead, this same merciful and loving God will see His people through. He always has, and He always will.

Tuck God's Word into your heart, and during times of distress, let it ring in your ears.

… God has said, "Never will I leave you; never will I forsake you." So we say with confidence, "The Lord is my helper; I will not be afraid. What can mere mortals do to me?"

(Hebrews 13:5b–6 NIV)

Thoughts to Ponder

Who will be delivered during this time of great distress? Does this mean no physical harm would come to them? See Daniel 12:1–4 and compare this scripture to Revelations 20:11–15.

_____

_____

_____

_____

What are the characteristics of those who will "shine like the brightness of the heavens" and "like the stars forever and ever"? (See Daniel 11:33–35 and Daniel 12:3,10.)

_____

_____

_____

_____

If wisdom is able to counter the forces of evil on this earth, how does one become wise? (See James 1:5.) Study further what James has to say about wisdom, particularly in James 1:2–7 and in James 3:13–18.

_____

_____

_____

_____

Chapter 28

The End Times— God's Love and Care

Scripture reference: Daniel 12:1–13 (NLT)

(This is the same passage as in Lesson 27, but we're looking at a different version to gain a broader perspective.)

(1) "At that time Michael, the archangel who stands guard over your nation, will arise. Then there will be a time of anguish greater than any since nations first came into existence. But at that time every one of your people whose name is written in the book will be rescued. (2) Many of those whose bodies lie dead and buried will rise up, some to everlasting life and some to shame and everlasting disgrace. (3) Those who are wise will shine as bright as the sky, and those who lead many to righteousness will shine like the stars forever. (4) But you, Daniel, keep this prophecy a secret; seal up the book until the time of the end, when many will rush here and there, and knowledge will increase."

(5) Then I, Daniel, looked and saw two others standing on opposite banks of the river. (6) One of them asked the man dressed in linen, who was now standing above the river, "How long will it be until these shocking events are over?"

(7) The man dressed in linen, who was standing above the river, raised both his hands toward heaven and took a solemn oath by the One who lives forever, saying, "It will go on for a time, times, and half a time. When the shattering of the holy people has finally come to an end, all these things will have happened."

(8) I heard what he said, but I did not understand what he meant. So I asked, "How will all this finally end, my lord?"

(9) But he said, "Go now, Daniel, for what I have said is kept secret and sealed until the time of the end. **(10)** Many will be purified, cleansed, and refined by these trials. But the wicked will continue in their wickedness, and none of them will understand. Only those who are wise will know what it means.

(11) "From the time the daily sacrifice is stopped and the sacrilegious object that causes desecration is set up to be worshiped, there will be 1,290 days. **(12)** And blessed are those who wait and remain until the end of the 1,335 days!

(13) "As for you, go your way until the end. You will rest, and then at the end of the days, you will rise again to receive the inheritance set aside for you."

As mentioned earlier, the Bible speaks of angels many times, but only two are identified by name—Michael and Gabriel. Both are mentioned in the book of Daniel. (Raphael and several other angels are mentioned in other writings. Satan and his followers are often referred to as "fallen angels.") Gabriel served as a messenger, while Michael is described as a protector of God's people in Daniel 12:1. When Michael is mentioned in the New Testament, he is seen directly confronting Satan in Jude 1:9 and Revelation 12:7.

What do the scriptures say about angels? They are powerful spiritual beings created by God. Although they seem to "work behind the scenes," at times they have appeared in a form visible to humans. They also have free will. Satan and his band of angels made the choice to oppose God. This group works to do us harm and seeks to turn us from God. Paul states in 2 Corinthians 11:14 that Satan himself masquerades as an angel of light. So it is important to remember that not all angels work for good.

The angels who have chosen to serve God provide yet another means for God to protect and care for His people. Although scriptures do not explain the full extent of their roles or exactly how they work, Jesus's statement in Matthew 18:10b (NASB) provides much comfort and insight. In talking about the little children, He stated, "… for I say to you that their angels in heaven continually see the face of My Father who is in heaven."

God continually covers His people with His love and care.

God's care is particularly evident in the book of Daniel, but as you read the Bible, you can see the great extent of His love and care for all the faithful. In some cases, He shows His love by sending angels to comfort and instruct chosen people. He also makes Himself available to each one of us, through Jesus and His Holy Spirit. Consider the many ways that God has shown, and continues to show, His great love and care for mankind:

- When He created Adam and Eve, He also *provided them a paradise* in which to live.
- When they chose to disobey, He had *already planned The Way* to restore mankind back to Himself. That Savior would be Jesus, who served as the perfect sacrifice for sin, once and for all.
- When Jesus fulfilled His mission on earth, He ascended back to heaven where He *continues His care for God's people*. He now sits at God's right hand, *interceding for us* (see Romans 8:34) and *serving as our high priest forever.* (See Hebrews 7:23–28.)
- So that the faithful would not be without an earthly Comforter, Jesus *sent the Holy Spirit to live within us*. "And I will pray the Father, and He will give you another Helper, that He may abide with you forever—the Spirit of truth, whom the world cannot receive, because it neither sees Him nor knows Him; but you know Him, for He dwells with you and will be in you" (John 14:16–17 NKJV).

- Paul states that the Holy Spirit also serves as a deposit, God's way of *guaranteeing the eternal life He has prepared for us*—"Now the one who has fashioned us for this very purpose is God, who has given us the Spirit as a deposit, guaranteeing what is to come" (2 Corinthians 5:5 NIV).
- Paul also explains how the Holy Spirit *intercedes for us*. "Likewise the Spirit helps us in our weakness. For we do not know what to pray for as we ought, but the Spirit himself intercedes for us with groanings too deep for words. And he who searches hearts knows what is the mind of the Spirit, because the Spirit intercedes for the saints according to the will of God" (Romans 8:26–27 ESV).
- Add to all this God's powerful angels, who *provide yet another layer to His care and protection*. Although they work in ways not fully understood, they wage battle against the forces of evil, both on earth and in the spiritual realms.

Truly, God surrounds His people, wrapping them completely with His love. Trials and tribulations on this earth continue today, but someday, they will come to an end. Remember that, come what may, God is there for you, providing His care and covering you with a love that never fails and never ceases. He will see you through.

"Trust in the Lord forever, for in God the Lord, we have an everlasting Rock."

(Isaiah 26:4 NASB)

Thoughts to Ponder

Evil will run its course here on this earth until the time of the end. Now, during this interim period, what will be going on with the faithful? With the wicked?

_____

_____

_____

_____

Daniel was elderly when he had this vision. Do you think he realized that almost everything mentioned in this vision would occur after his death?

_____

_____

_____

_____

What assurance was Daniel given in Daniel 12:13? How does this scripture provide assurance to us today?

_____

_____

_____

_____

Chapter 29

The Meaning of the Visions of Daniel

Scripture reference: Daniel 12:1–13 (MSG)

(This is the same passage as in Lessons 27 and 28, but we're looking at a third version to learn even more.)

(1–2) "That's when Michael, the great angel-prince, champion of your people, will step in. It will be a time of trouble, the worst trouble the world has ever seen. But your people will be saved from the trouble, every last one found written in the Book. Many who have been long dead and buried will wake up, some to eternal life, others to eternal shame.

(3) "Men and women who have lived wisely and well will shine brilliantly, like the cloudless, star-strewn night skies. And those who put others on the right path to life will glow like stars forever.

(4) "This is a confidential report, Daniel, for your eyes and ears only. Keep it secret. Put the book under lock and key until the end. In the interim there is going to be a lot of frantic running around, trying to figure out what's going on."

(5–6) As I, Daniel, took all this in, two figures appeared, one standing on this bank of the river and one on the other bank. One of them asked a third man who was dressed in linen and who straddled the river, "How long is this astonishing story to go on?"

(7) The man dressed in linen, who straddled the river, raised both hands to the skies. I heard him solemnly swear by the Eternal One that it would be a time, two times, and half a time, that when the oppressor of the holy people was brought down the story would be complete.

(8) I heard all this plainly enough, but I didn't understand it. So I asked, "Master, can you explain this to me?"

(9–10) "Go on about your business, Daniel," he said. "The message is confidential and under lock and key until the end, until things are about to be wrapped up. The populace will be washed clean and made like new. But the wicked will just keep on being wicked, without a clue about what is happening. Those who live wisely and well will understand what's going on.

(11–13) "From the time that the daily worship is banished from the Temple and the obscene desecration is set up in its place, there will be 1,290 days. Blessed are those who patiently make it through the 1,335 days. And you? Go about your business without fretting or worrying. Relax. When it's all over, you will be on your feet to receive your reward."

This rich passage of scripture holds so many treasures that it bears examining yet another time. Different translations can provide insights that might have been missed in another.

The visions in the book of Daniel are presented in a literary style often referred to as *apocalyptic*. This word is a derivation of *apocalypse*, meaning a prediction of looming disaster or the final doom of the world. Like other prophetic writings, these visions foretell the future but often use symbols and imagery that are strange or unknown.

Visions, like dreams, paint a picture. Pictures are often so much more effective for human understanding than just presenting a list of facts. Years of information can be condensed and the meaning conveyed quickly using pictures. Although

Daniel couldn't grasp every detail, this vision from God effectively revealed to him the big picture.

What would have happened if Daniel *had* understood all the details? As wise and as educated and as connected to God as Daniel was, the awesomeness and complexity of what he saw often overwhelmed him. After the vision that's recorded in Daniel 8, he lay exhausted for several days before being able to get up and go back to work (verse 27).

God's thoughts are higher than human thoughts.

Yes, Daniel's visions often perplexed him. He knew he was seeing only the tip of the iceberg. So much more lay beyond the limited understanding his human mind could hold. Merely glimpsing the enormity of God's thoughts overwhelmed him.

As history has unfolded, various happenings seem to align with those foretold in Daniel's visions, but much will simply remain uncertain until the end of time. Like Daniel, people today don't have to fully understand the prophecies to appreciate them.

With that being said, be sure not to miss the wonderful messages which *can* be understood:
- There will be a resurrection of the dead, and everyone whose name is written in the Book will be saved. (See Daniel 12:2–3.) This promise was not only for those living under the Old Law but has also been repeated in the New Testament for Christians today in Revelation 20:12.
- The populace will be washed clean and made like new. (See Daniel 12:10.) The blood of Jesus did that for all the righteous who lived before Him and for all who would live after. (See Hebrews 9:15, 25–28.)
- God will take care of things. Like Daniel, the faithful today should live their lives without worrying about how the end events will unfold. (See Daniel 12:13.)

Thank goodness God is so much bigger than humans, so much bigger than all of His creation. While the mind of God is beyond understanding, know that you can, with all certainty, trust in Him and in His promises.

Do you not know? Have you not heard?

The Everlasting God, the Lord, the Creator of the ends of the earth

Does not become weary or tired.

His understanding is inscrutable.

He gives strength to the weary,

And to him who lacks might He increases power.

Though youths grow weary and tired,

And vigorous young men stumble badly,

Yet those who wait for the Lord

Will gain new strength;

They will mount up with wings like eagles,

They will run and not get tired,

They will walk and not become weary.
(Isaiah 40:28–31 NASB)

Thoughts to Ponder

What is the significance of the linen garment of "the man dressed in linen"? Who do you think this man is?

_____

_____

_____

_____

When you read Daniel 12 in this version (The Message), do you sense that we are not supposed to fully understand the meaning of this vision? (See verses 4 and 9.)

_____

_____

_____

_____

Although it's interesting to read what various scholars have to say about the meaning of Daniel's visions, what are your important take-aways from reading and studying this vision, particularly the explanation given to Daniel in Chapter 12?

_____

_____

_____

_____

Chapter 30

Daniel—A Righteous and Wise Man of God

Aside from the Old Testament book bearing his name, the prophet Daniel is mentioned several times by his contemporary, the prophet Ezekiel. Although Daniel is not the subject of the passages below, they're interesting to study.

God called Ezekiel when he was thirty years old and gave him this charge: "Son of man, I have made you a watchman for the people of Israel; so hear the word I speak and give them warning from me" (Ezekiel 3:17 NIV). A watchman was someone appointed to keep a sharp vigil and sound the trumpet to warn of impending danger. From the tone of his writings, you can hear Ezekiel sounding the alarm loud and clear as he relayed God's messages.[1]

1

Ezekiel in Exile. This article provides information on "Tel Abib" in Babylonia where Ezekiel went during the exile. Scroll down to see a map of the Persian Empire.

bit.ly/2lou0b2

Ezekiel 14:12–20 (NIV)

(12) The word of the Lord came to me: **(13)** "Son of man, if a country sins against me by being unfaithful and I stretch out my hand against it to cut off its food supply and send famine upon it and kill its people and their animals, **(14)** even if these three men—Noah, **Daniel** and Job—were in it, they could save only themselves by their righteousness, declares the Sovereign Lord.

(15) "Or if I send wild beasts through that country and they leave it childless and it becomes desolate so that no one can pass through it because of the beasts, (16) as surely as I live, declares the Sovereign Lord, even if these three men were in it, they could not save their own sons or daughters. They alone would be saved, but the land would be desolate.

(17) "Or if I bring a sword against that country and say, 'Let the sword pass throughout the land,' and I kill its people and their animals, (18) as surely as I live, declares the Sovereign Lord, even if these three men were in it, they could not save their own sons or daughters. They alone would be saved.

(19) "Or if I send a plague into that land and pour out my wrath on it through bloodshed, killing its people and their animals, (20) as surely as I live, declares the Sovereign Lord, even if Noah, **Daniel** and Job were in it, they could save neither son nor daughter. They would save only themselves by their righteousness."

Ezekiel 28:1–3 (NIV)

(1) The word of the Lord came to me: (2) "Son of man, say to the ruler of Tyre, 'This is what the Sovereign Lord says:

"'In the pride of your heart you say, "I am a god;

I sit on the throne of a god in the heart of the seas."

But you are a mere mortal and not a god, though you think you are as wise as a god.

(3) Are you wiser than **Daniel**? Is no secret hidden from you?'"

In both of these passages, God issues His warnings concerning the dire consequences which are to come. In the first, He refers to Noah, Daniel and Job, men who would have been well known to the Israelites. He holds them up as representing the highest caliber of righteousness, and not even they will be able to change His mind in the matters He is addressing.

Job was the epitome of a righteous person, who remained faithful despite the devastating circumstances that kept coming at him. Noah's righteousness saved him and his family from destruction, keeping mankind alive on the earth. By naming Daniel alongside men of such renown, God shows the great esteem He holds for him.

In the second passage, God again affirms His high regard for Daniel. The city and the king of Tyre had all grown arrogant, and worse, prideful over Jerusalem's miseries. God called out the king, essentially saying to him—just who do you think you are? He held up Daniel in comparison as a person of great wisdom, someone the king of Tyre would likely have known about due to Daniel's prominent position in Babylonia.

God's Word Is True.

While Daniel is only mentioned in passing in this scripture, the prophecy concerning Tyre and its king is not only interesting to read but also attests to the truth of God's Word. The entire prophecy is quite lengthy, particularly in comparison to the judgments proclaimed against other nations. (See Ezekiel 26, 27, and 28). Why did God go into such detail? Well, it's one thing for a person or a nation to sin, but to taunt God or to revel in the suffering of His people is particularly offensive to God.

Those of us living today can read this ancient prophecy and see how it came true as the centuries passed. Situated on an island off the Phoenician coast, this long-established, wealthy and prominent city considered itself virtually impregnable against invading forces. Yet, as God had decreed, Tyre endured one siege after another from various nations.

Finally, its rulers rebuffed someone who absolutely would not be denied, Alexander the Great. He literally tore down the city of Old Tyre located on the mainland and used the great amount of rubble to build a causeway to the island city of Tyre. In 332 BC, some 200 plus years after Ezekiel's prophecy, Alexander the

---
2

3 Good Reasons to Believe the Bible Is from God. This interesting article discusses the destruction of the Phoenician city of Tyre as foretold by the prophet Ezekiel.

bit.ly/2IQcZYk

Tyre in Prophecy. This article provides more information about this ancient city and its defeat by Alexander the Great.

bit.ly/1qx37dx

Maps of Tyre:

Now and Then. This map depicts what the island city looked like before Alexander the Great laid siege. It includes the present day coastline to show how it has changed.

bit.ly/2kOBBg0

Map of the Siege of Tyre. This map depicts the Siege of Tyre, 333–332 BC.

bit.ly/2kOFFwL

Great conquered Tyre. In so doing, he caused the topography to be forever altered. With sand and silt continuing to build up through the centuries, the causeway he created actually turned the island into a peninsula.[2]

> Therefore this is what the Sovereign Lord says: "I am against you, Tyre, and I will bring many nations against you, like the sea casting up its waves. They will destroy the walls of Tyre and pull down her towers; I will scrape away her rubble and make her a bare rock. Out in the sea she will become a place to spread fishnets, for I have spoken, declares the Sovereign Lord. She will become plunder for the nations, and her settlements on the mainland will be ravaged by the sword. Then they will know that I am the Lord."
>
> (Ezekiel 26:3–6 NIV)

Later, when the Jewish traveler, Benjamin of Tudela, published his diary in approximately AD 1170, he commented, "A man can ascend the walls of New Tyre and see ancient Tyre, which the sea has now covered, lying at a stone's throw from the new city. And should one care to go forth by boat, one can see the castles, market-places, streets, and palaces in the bed of the sea."[3]

For the word of the Lord is right and true; he is faithful in all he does. The Lord loves righteousness and justice; the earth is full of his unfailing love.

(Psalm 33:4–5 NIV)

3

The Itinerary of Benjamin of Tudela. Using the Find function on your keyboard, search this ancient text for "Tyre." You'll find the quoted reference where it's marked p. 30 and p. 31 within the text. If you click "See Other Formats" in the top right corner, you can view the text in book form, where you can find maps from the 1100's right before the title page.

bit.ly/2kJs1ew

Using maps.google.com or another search engine, pull up a current map of Tyre, Lebanon, to see what the area looks like today. Check out the aerial satellite view as well.

Thoughts to Ponder

Why do you suppose God specifically named Noah, Daniel and Job in these scriptures?

_____
_____
_____
_____

What does it say about Daniel that he is named along with Noah and Job? What does it say about him that he is mentioned in the prophecy against the king of Tyre?

_____
_____
_____
_____

For an interesting study, read Ezekiel's prophecies against Tyre in Ezekiel 26–28 and then research the history of the city and the region. Look at the maps of ancient Tyre and see how Alexander the Great permanently altered the area.

_____
_____
_____
_____

Chapter 31

Daniel—A Prophet of God

In the New Testament, Daniel is specifically mentioned only once, by Jesus Himself. The disciples had come to Jesus privately as He was sitting on the Mount of Olives and asked Him how they would know when the end of the age had come. Jesus references the prophecy of Daniel in His reply.

Matthew 24:1–21 (NLT)

(1) As Jesus was leaving the Temple grounds, his disciples pointed out to him the various Temple buildings. **(2)** But he responded, "Do you see all these buildings? I tell you the truth, they will be completely demolished. Not one stone will be left on top of another!"

(3) Later, Jesus sat on the Mount of Olives. His disciples came to him privately and said, "Tell us, when will all this happen? What sign will signal your return and the end of the world?"

(4) Jesus told them, "Don't let anyone mislead you, **(5)** for many will come in my name, claiming, 'I am the Messiah.' They will deceive many. **(6)** And you will hear of wars and threats of wars, but don't panic. Yes, these things must take place, but the end won't follow immediately. **(7)** Nation will go to war against nation, and kingdom against kingdom. There will be famines and earthquakes in many parts of the world. **(8)** But all this is only the first of the birth pains, with more to come.

(9) "Then you will be arrested, persecuted, and killed. You will be hated all over the world because you are my followers. **(10)** And many will turn away from me and betray and hate each other. **(11)** And many false prophets will appear and will deceive many people. **(12)** Sin will be rampant everywhere, and the love of many will grow cold. **(13)** But the one who endures to the end will be saved. **(14)** And the Good News about the Kingdom will be preached throughout the whole world, so that all nations will hear it; and then the end will come.

(15) "The day is coming when you will see what **Daniel** the prophet spoke about—the sacrilegious object that causes desecration standing in the Holy Place." (Reader, pay attention!) **(16)** "Then those in Judea must flee to the hills. **(17)** A person out on the deck of a roof must not go down into the house to pack. **(18)** A person out in the field must not return even to get a coat. **(19)** How terrible it will be for pregnant women and for nursing mothers in those days. **(20)** And pray that your flight will not be in winter or on the Sabbath. **(21)** For there will be greater anguish than at any time since the world began. And it will never be so great again."

Jesus spoke many times of things His disciples did not understand. It was not unusual for them to ask Him to explain His words. This time, however, instead of illustrating a lesson or principle with a parable, Jesus prophesied and told them of future events. And what an incredible prophecy it was—almost too much for them to imagine or bear.

The temple in Jerusalem was sacred to the Jews. It was the dwelling place of God Himself. The people had endured its destruction before, when Nebuchadnezzar had desecrated it and carried the Jews who lived through his sieges off into Babylonian captivity. Now, Jesus's disciples were hearing that the temple would again be destroyed.

This destruction would be so extensive that not one stone would be left stacked upon another. Moreover, the forces of destruction would be so great that many of the people would be persecuted and killed, while those left alive would flee for their very lives. The distress upon the Jewish people would be the greatest they had even known, so great that it would mark the end of the era.

Indeed, in AD 70, the Romans laid siege on Jerusalem. Their great slaughter of the Jews was so merciless and so gruesome that blood ran down the temple steps. The temple itself was burned and plundered, and the city of Jerusalem was almost completely destroyed. The Jewish historian, Josephus Flavius, recorded first-hand this incredible Roman assault on the temple.[1]

Why did this great destruction have to occur? The center of Jewish religion was Jerusalem, with the temple providing a conduit to God. However, the people had failed to follow God as He had commanded. Remember Jesus's lament in Matthew 23:37 (ESV), "O Jerusalem, Jerusalem, the city that kills the prophets and stones those who are sent to it! How often would I have gathered your children together as a hen gathers her brood under her wings, and you were not willing!" The destruction of Jerusalem and the earthly temple forcefully brought an end to the old era and helped usher in the new.

Daniel was a prophet of God.

It is only fitting that Jesus quoted Daniel in this scripture, as the prophecies conveyed through Daniel largely dealt with the coming of Christ. Jesus himself was the fulfillment of much of what Daniel's visions of the future had foretold. Additionally, Daniel was recognized as a man of God by his contemporaries, both the Jews and the Babylonians. Here, Jesus further validates Daniel by referencing his prophecies.

What do these prophecies foretold so long ago mean for people living today? You can know that, from the beginning, God planned a Way of Salvation for you. Even though sin separates you from Him, He desires a relationship with you so much that He planned a means to bridge that separation. The Old

---
1

Refer to the articles referenced in Lesson 26 and Lesson 27.

Law provided a temporary means, with atonement for sin being made over and over. Jesus fulfilled the Old Law and became a permanent atonement, offering Himself as the perfect sacrifice for sin, once and for all. The really good news? God's chosen people are no longer defined by someone's earthly lineage, but rather by whether they believe and obey God's Word!

These prophecies also show how God keeps His promises. He does what He says He will do. With certainty, Christians today can cling to the promises He has made time and again through the ages to His faithful.

… God has said, "Never will I leave you; never will I forsake you." So we say with confidence, "The Lord is my helper; I will not be afraid. What can mere mortals do to me?"

(Hebrews 13:5b–6 NIV)

And to that, may we all say—Amen.
Come, Lord Jesus!

Thoughts to Ponder

How does Jesus's prophecy concerning the near future correspond with what Daniel had prophesied over 500 years earlier?

_____

_____

_____

_____

Jesus's disciples had likely heard or read the scripture in the book of Daniel to which Jesus referred. How do you think they felt upon hearing Jesus tell them these things were going to occur soon?

_____

_____

_____

_____

The discovery of the Dead Sea Scrolls have further affirmed both the contents of the book of Daniel and the date around which it was written. How do these scrolls, along with other historical records, attest to the divine inspiration of the scriptures?

_____

_____

_____

_____

Also by Marilynn E. Hood

Moses: Called By God
Living by Faith through the Journeys of Life

God's call on your life may seem impossible.
And maybe you've thought . . .

I'm not the one for the job.
I don't know how to do what You're asking me to do.
It's simply too much.
I'm exhausted by my responsibilities.

You aren't alone. When God called Moses to lead His people out of slavery, Moses begged God to choose someone else. Who could blame him? The job God had given Moses was massive! It seemed impossible. But God never expected Moses to do it alone.

Called by God to an extraordinary, life-changing journey, Moses led a fledgling nation of doubtful and often discontented people to the Promised Land. Along the way, he faced incredible challenges and disappointments. Moses also discovered a truth that remains today: God offers incomparable love and mercy to those who follow Him.

This study of Moses's life focuses on the relationship he had with God, a relationship he did not ask for or expect. Moses learned to trust God's goodness and faithfulness, and he experienced the kind of closeness that God desires to have with you today.

"Moses's story offers a gentle reminder to be listening for those burning bush moments when God can clarify our purpose and calling."

—**Dan Miller**, *New York Times* bestselling author of *48 Days to the Work You Love*, and host of the 48 Days Podcast

"The insights and questions Marilynn offers help us understand that, like Moses, we can experience a deep and extraordinary relationship with God, which is exactly what He created us for!"

—**Meredith Perryman**, speaker, Bible teacher, and author of *The Whole Story*

"If you're wondering if God has called you or what His purpose is for you, this reflective study will help you find the answers."

—**Bill Rieser**, pastor, author, evangelist, and founder of Encounter Ministries

"Bible students and teachers alike will find lots of helpful information and inspiration in *Moses: Called by God*."
—**Debbie W. Wilson**, author of *Little Strength, Big God*

MarilynnHood.com/moses
info@courageousheartpress.com

Resources

Setting the Scene

1. Russell, Rusty, "Historical and Biblical Time Chart," *Bible History Online,* bible-history.com/resource/r_time.htm.

Bratcher, Dennis, "Israelite Kings Date Chart," *Christian Resource Institute,* 2015, crivoice.org/israelitekings.html.

Deffinbaugh, Bob, "21. The Great Divorce: The Kingdom Divided (1 Kings 12; 2 Chronicles 10)," *From Creation to the Cross. Bible.org*, Feb. 16, 2007, bible.org/seriespage/21-great-divorce-kingdom-divided-1-kings-12-2-chronicles-10.

Hooker, Richard. "The Hebrews: a Learning Module," *Washington State University*, quoted in "Ancient Jewish History: The Two Kingdoms." *Jewish Virtual Library*, jewishvirtuallibrary.org/jsource/History/Kingdoms1.html.

"The Babylonian Captivity with Map: Timeline of Events," *Bible History Online,* 2003, bible-history.com/map_babylonian_captivity/map_of_the_deportation_of_judah_timeline_of_events.html.

"The Babylonian Captivity with Map: The Destruction of Jerusalem," *Bible History Online*, 2016, bible-history.com/map_babylonian_captivity/map_of_the_deportation_of_judah_the_destruction_of_jerusalem.html.

Chapter 1: A Message from God

1. "Bible Timeline: Old Testament," *Bible Hub*, biblehub.com/timeline/old.htm.

"The Rulers and Prophets of Daniel's Time," *Truthnet.org,* truthnet.org/Daniel/Introduction/danieltimeline1.JPG.

2. "The Babylonian Captivity (with map)," *Bible History Online*, 2016, bible-history.com/map_babylonian_captivity/.

Russell, R., "Ancient Babylonia," *Bible History Online,* 2016, bible-history.com/babylonia/.

3. Tissot, James Jacques Joseph (French, 1836–1902), "The Flight of the Prisoners," gouache on board, c. 1896–1902 (Jewish Museum, New York, NY), commons.wikimedia.org/wiki/File:Tissot_The_Flight_of_the_Prisoners.jpg.

Chapter 2: Living in Times of Turbulence

1. Padfield, David, "Carchemish, and the Major Battle of 606 BCE," Edited by Fred P. Miller, *MoellerHaus Publisher,* 2016, moellerhaus.com/Jeremiah/battleCarchemish.html.

Chapter 3: Living under Someone Else's Control

1. Baker, Luke, "Ancient tablets reveal life of Jews in Nebuchadnezzar's Babylon," *Reuters.com*, Feb. 3, 2015, reut.rs/2kTbyXs.

Chapter 4: Nurtured by God in a Foreign Land

1. Campbell, Mike, "Patrick," *Behind the Name,* 2017, behindthename.com.

Hitchcock, Floyd. "Chapter 2–Daniel, Hananiah, Mishael and Azariah–The Name Changes." *The March of Empires–Lectures on the Book of Daniel,* 1944, *Baptist Bible Believer's Website*, bit.ly/2li6GfB.

Chapter 14: King Belshazzar Sees the Writing on the Wall

1. Jastrow, Jr., Morris, Ira Maurice Price, Marcus Jastrow, and H. M. Speaker, "Belshazzar," *Jewish Encyclopedia,* 1906, jewishencyclopedia.com/articles/2846-belshazzar.

Chapter 16: King Darius Regrets His Decree

1. Jackson, Wayne, "Nero Caesar and the Christian Faith," *ChristianCourier.com*, Access date: February 13, 2017, christiancourier.com/articles/623-nero-caesar-and-the-christian-faith.

Chapter 20: Daniel's Vision of the Ram and the Goat

1. Bracefield, Sue, "Worship in the Early Church," *Grace Theological College*, New Zealand, gtc.ac.nz/Files/Publications/Articles/Early%20Christian%20Worship.pdf.

Chapter 21: Daniel's Second Vision Explained

1. Deffinbaugh, Bob, "9. The Ram, the Goat, and the Horn (Daniel 8:1–27)," *Daniel: Relating Prophecy to Piety, Bible.org,* May 26, 2004, bible.org/seriespage/ram-goat-and-horn-daniel-81-27.

Mark, Joshua J., "Susa," *Ancient History Encyclopedia,* Sept. 2, 2009, ancient.eu/susa.

"The Babylonian Captivity with Map: Susa," *Bible History Online,* bible-history.com/map_babylonian_captivity/map_of_the_deportation_of_judah_susa.html.

Chapter 26: Difficult Times for God's People

1. "1 Maccabees 1," *Douay-Rheims 1899 American Edition Bible*, *Bible Gateway*, biblegateway.com/passage/?search=1+Maccabees+1&version=DRA.

Josephus, Flavius, *War of the Jews,* Book 1, Chapter 1, Paragraph 2, *Bible Study Tools*, biblestudytools.com/history/flavius-josephus/war-of-the-jews/book-1/chapter-1.html.

Chapter 27: The End Times—Great Changes to Come

1. "The Romans Destroy the Temple at Jerusalem, 70 AD," *EyeWitness to History*, 2005, eyewitnesstohistory.com/jewishtemple.htm.

Schaff, Philip, "The Jewish War and the Destruction of Jerusalem, AD 70," *The History of the Christian Church, Volume 1*, *Bible Hub*. biblehub.com/library/schaff/history_of_the_christian_church_volume_i/section_38_the_jewish_war.htm.

Chapter 30: Daniel—A Righteous and Wise Man of God

1. "The Babylonian Captivity: Tel Abib," *Bible History Online*, bible-history.com/map_babylonian_captivity/map_of_the_deportation_of_judah_tel_abib.html.

2. Lyons, Eric and Kyle Butt. "3 Good Reasons to Believe the Bible Is from God." *Apologetics Press*, apologeticspress.org/APContent.aspx?category=13&article=5089&topic=283.

Butt, Kyle, "Tyre in Prophecy," *Apologetics Press*, apologeticspress.org/apcontent.aspx?category=13&article=1790.

"Historical Map of Tyre," Hammond Inc., Maplewood, N.J., *EmersonKent.com*, emersonkent.com/map_archive/tyre.htm.

"Historical Map of Type and Vicinity: Illustrating the Siege of Tyre, 333–332 BC," United States Military Academy Department of History, *EmersonKent.com*, emersonkent.com/map_archive/siege_of_tyre.htm.

3. Adler, Marcus Nathan. *The Itinerary of Benjamin of Tudela: Critical Text, Translation and Commentary* (New York: Philipp Feldheim, Inc., 1907), 30-31, bit.ly/2oWXMIL.

For Further Study

These reference materials provide a great deal of information that may be of interest:

Bible Gateway—This site makes the Bible available in a variety of different languages, versions, and translations. It also provides search tools, reading plans, devotionals and Bible reference works. To find a listing of the books of the Bible, click on "Bible Book List" right under the search bar.
biblegateway.com

Bible History Online—This comprehensive site provides a multitude of maps, articles, images, and resources.
bible-history.com

Christian Classics Ethereal Library—Browse this extensive collection of online Christian works.
ccel.org

Tomb of Daniel—This shrine was built to honor Daniel in Susa, Iran, but his bones seem to have been moved numerous times through the centuries and their exact whereabouts evidently cannot be verified.
en.wikipedia.org/wiki/Tomb_of_Daniel

About the Author

Marilynn E. Hood is a Christian who has studied the Bible for most of her life. She draws upon her own personal learning journey and years of teaching experience in presenting these lessons from the book of Daniel.

Marilynn holds an MBA from Texas A&M University, where she later joined the faculty in the Department of Finance and taught the principles of personal finance to thousands of students. She also taught the principles of insurance in the CERTIFIED FINANCIAL PLANNER™ Program offered by Texas A&M University's Department of Agricultural Economics.

Marilynn is the author of *Money for Life* and *Moses: Called by God*. Having retired from university teaching, she and her husband of fifty-two years, David Hood, currently reside on their farm near Bryan, Texas. They are the parents of three children and, more importantly, the grandparents to six wonderful grandchildren and one adorable great-granddaughter.

www.ingramcontent.com/pod-product-compliance
Lightning Source LLC
Chambersburg PA
CBHW060455300426
44113CB00016B/2602